CarTech®, Inc.
838 Lake Street South
Forest Lake, MN 55025
Phone: 651-277-1200 or 800-551-4754
Fax: 651-277-1203
www.cartechbooks.com

© 2016 by Art Evans

All rights reserved. No part of this publication may be reproduced or utilized in any form or by any means, electronic or mechanical, including photocopying, recording, or by any information storage and retrieval system, without prior permission from the Publisher. All text, photographs, and artwork are the property of the Author unless otherwise noted or credited.

The information in this work is true and complete to the best of our knowledge. However, all information is presented without any guarantee on the part of the Author or Publisher, who also disclaim any liability incurred in connection with the use of the information and any implied warranties of merchantability or fitness for a particular purpose. Readers are responsible for taking suitable and appropriate safety measures when performing any of the operations or activities described in this work.

All trademarks, trade names, model names and numbers, and other product designations referred to herein are the property of their respective owners and are used solely for identification purposes. This work is a publication of CarTech, Inc., and has not been licensed, approved, sponsored, or endorsed by any other person or entity. The Publisher is not associated with any product, service, or vendor mentioned in this book, and does not endorse the products or services of any vendor mentioned in this book.

Edit by Bob Wilson
Layout by Monica Seiberlich

ISBN 978-1-61325-460-8
Item No. CT650

Library of Congress Cataloging-in-Publication Data

Names: Evans, Arthur G., author.
Title: Carroll Shelby : a collection of my favorite racing photos / Art Evans.
Description: Forest Lake, MN : CarTech, [2016]
Identifiers: LCCN 2016003466 | ISBN 9781613253229
Subjects: LCSH: Shelby, Carroll, 1923-2012. | Automobile racing drivers–United States–Biography. | Automobile racing drivers–United States–Pictorial works. | Automobiles, Racing.
Classification: LCC GV1032.S5 E83 2016 | DDC 796.720922 [B] –dc23
LC record available at https://lccn.loc.gov/2016003466

Written, edited, and designed in the U.S.A.
Printed in China
10 9 8 7 6 5 4 3 2 1

Front Cover: *The Los Angeles Region staged an SCCA National at Palm Springs on November 4, 1956. Shelby drove a Ferrari 410 in the race. Soon, the race developed into an intense duel between Shelby and Phil Hill. The two were never more than fractions of a second apart. They had the crowd of more than 30,000 spectators standing. After an hour and a half of intense racing, Starter Al Torres dropped the checkered flag on Shelby with Hill still close behind. Shelby celebrated his win with the Race Queen, Miss Palm Springs Stephanie Bruton, and Phil Hill.*

Endpapers: *The Aston Martin team at Sebring on March 7, 1954. Shelby is in front of the third car looking down. He was teamed with Charlie Wallace. They were running with the first six overall when the rear axle broke, putting them out of the race. Still impressed with Shelby, John Wyer suggested he go to England and that there might be a place for him on the Aston team.*

Frontispiece: *Shelby's time at Bonneville led Donald Healey to ask Carroll to drive in the Carrera Panamericana (the Mexican Road Race) that started on November 18, 1954. One of the most difficult and demanding races in the world, the route covered 1,932 miles from the south of Mexico at Tuxtla Guttierez to the north at Ciudad Juarez. This photo by* Motor Trend *photographer Bob D'Olivo shows Shelby at the start with officials and crew.*

Title Page: *Shelby makes a pit stop at the 1956 Sebring. Carroll and Roy Salvadori finished 4th overall and 1st in Class D. The other two Astons failed to finish. Juan Manuel Fangio and Eugenio Castellotti won in a 3.5-liter Ferrari. In 2nd were Luigi Musso and Harry Schell in another Ferrari followed by Bob Sweikert and Jack Ensley in a D-Type Jaguar. Shelby and Salvadori were eight laps behind the winner at the end.*

Table of Contents: *"The high-point of my driving career was when Roy Salvadori and I won Le Mans in 1959." Shelby celebrated the Le Mans victory with his crew and David Brown, opening a bottle of champagne. It was also a victory for Brown as it was the only Le Mans win for Aston Martin.*

Back Cover Photos

Top: *Shelby's Las Vegas factory continues to turn out Cobras as well as Shelby Mustangs, with new models announced every year. The Ford factory ships Mustangs to Las Vegas where they are transformed into Shelbys. A Shelby Mustang is the top of the line at selected Ford dealers. The legendary Shelby Mustang GT-H (originally made for Hertz) was resurrected in 2006.*

Bottom: *The last and most important race of the Bahamas Speed Week was the Nassau Trophy on December 7. Stirling Moss (left) won in a 3.5 Ferrari followed by Shelby (center) in the Maserati and Phil Hill (right) in a 4.1 Ferrari. Nassau chairman "Red" Crise stands behind them.*

Author note: Some of the vintage photos in this book are of lower quality. They have been included because of their importance to telling the story.

OVERSEAS DISTRIBUTION BY:

PGUK
63 Hatton Garden
London EC1N 8LE, England
Phone: 020 7061 1980 • Fax: 020 7242 3725
www.pguk.co.uk

Renniks Publications Ltd.
3/37-39 Green Street
Banksmeadow, NSW 2109, Australia
Phone: 2 9695 7055 • Fax: 2 9695 7355
www.renniks.com

Table of Contents

Preface by Carroll Shelby

This book is the story of my life: I was born in 1923 in Texas. After flying bombers in World War II, I raced during the 1950s, winning the SCCA National Championship, Le Mans, and the USAC Sports Car Championship.

During the 1960s, I opened a driving school and produced Cobras, King Cobras, and Shelby Mustangs. My cars won everything there was to win including the FIA Manufacturers' Championship. My team ran Ford GTs and won the triple crown of racing in 1966: Daytona, Sebring, and Le Mans as well as the Manufacturers' Championship for Ford. In my spare time, I invented my very own Chili and sold it to Kraft Foods.

During the 1980s, I produced modified versions of Dodges and in 1990, got a new heart. In 1999, I built my own sports car, the Series I, from the ground up. I also began building more Cobras and Shelby Mustangs in my factory in Las Vegas.

Preface by Art Evans

As you read this book, remember that there are two authors: Carroll Shelby and I. *Shelby's words are in italics*, while mine are not. Carroll Shelby and I were close friends for many years. I called him "Shel." A few years ago, I made arrangements for him to publish a book about his family. Then he wanted a new edition of his book *The Cobra Story* and I helped him with that. So we started talking about a publishing partnership. Our first was my book *The Shelby American Story*.

Then he decided that he wanted to try to memorialize the story of his life. During his later years, however, his eyesight deteriorated and he found it difficult to read. But he did enjoy looking at pictures. So we started working together gathering photographs to tell his life story. His daughter, Sharon, contributed a number of them from his early life. And there were many in the archives of his companies.

In addition, many friends contributed photographs that they had taken or that were from their collections: Paul-Henri Cahier, Ginny and John Dixon, Bob D'Olivo, Will Edgar, Cliff Emmich, David Evans, Joel Finn, Dave Friedman, Jim Gessner, Carl Goodwin, Vince Howlett, Steve Johnson, Allen Kuhn, Pete Lyons, Karl Ludvigsen, Don Meacham, Peter Miles, Bill Neale, Willem Oosthoek, Lynn Park, Ken Parker, John Persselin, Rich Sparkman, Jim Sitz, Tracy Smith, Bob Tronolone, and Gordon Whitby. I think I speak for Shel when I say, "Thank you all."

Also my sincere thanks to the staff at CarTech for the outstanding job they have done in bringing Shelby's story to life.

So we started to put together his picture story, his scrapbook, as it were. Unfortunately, Shelby died before we finished. Nevertheless, after a period of mourning and depression, I completed it. I wrote some of the text. For the rest, I recorded Shel and used his words; in these cases, it's in italics.

Special thanks to Ginny Dixon (proofreader par excellence) as well as Tracey Smith, John Dixon, and, most of all, Don Klein, who is one of the very best motorsports journalists; all have reviewed this story.

Growing Up

"My first car."

Shelby's father worked for the U.S. Postal Service.
Sometimes young Carroll accompanied him.
That's Carroll looking out of the window.

He recalled, "*Dad was a rural mail carrier, but contrary to what one might think, he made out pretty well at it. My earliest recollection is that he got around in a buggy in East Texas. Delivering mail was pretty hard work; he would be out from early in the morning until late at night.*"

Carroll Hall Shelby was born on January 11, 1923, in Texas. His father was Warren Hall Shelby who was born in 1897 in Texas and died in 1943. His mother was Francis Eloise Lawrence, born in 1903 in Texas and died in 1951. They married on April 7, 1922.

Carroll Hall Shelby was born on January 11, 1923, in Texas.

During the 1930s, the Shelby family lived in this house in the small Texas town of Leesburg.

Growing Up

Carroll had one sister, Lula Anne, who was born in 1926. She was also born in Leesburg, Texas. *"There was just the two of us and, since there weren't many other children around where we lived, we spent a lot of time playing together."*

This formal portrait of Shelby was taken when he was 14.

Shelby remembered that his dad had a succession of cars.

"I couldn't wait to have one of my own, which I did when I was 15 years old. When I talk about having owned a car at that age, I'm kind of overstating the facts. Actually, it was my dad's car, but he let me spend so much time with his investment that I got to thinking of it as my own."

Growing Up

A teenage Carroll with his mother, Francis Eloise, and sister, Lula.

This portrait was taken with his mother when he was a few years older.

In the Service

"When World War II came along, I joined the Army Air Corps."

"After training, I got my wings and was commissioned as a second lieutenant in 1942."

1942

Shelby is second from the left.
I have been unable to identify
the others.

"I trained in AT-11s flying over Texas."

In the Service

"On December 18, 1944, I married my
high-school sweetheart, Jeanne Fields,
while I was still in the Air Corps."

In the Service

"After flying B-18 bombers, I graduated to B-25s, B-26s, and finally B-29s."

It was the practice of the Air Corps during World War II to keep the very best pilots in the United States to train others. So Shelby, although he requested it, never went into combat.

In the Service

Carroll and Jeanne's first offspring was Sharon Ann,
born on September 27, 1944.

Shelby is at the far right. Again,
I was unable to identify the others.

"My last assignment was flying B-29s out of Lowry Air Corps Base near Denver, Colorado.
After the war ended in 1945, I was mustered out, still a second lieutenant."

In the Service

Shelby remembered, *"All during 1948 and part of 1949 I worked in the oil fields, putting in a lot of hard labor and getting little pay in return."*

BERT FIELDS
B C HUMPHREY NO 2
H&TC SURVEY JONES CO

In the meantime, he and Jeanne had their first son, Michael Hall, in 1946.

In the Service

This snapshot, from Sharon's collection,
is of his chicken ranch.

In the Service

When Shelby quit the oil business, he went into the chicken business. At first, he did well and made a lot of money. As he remembered, *"I started raising 20,000 at a time and really worked at it. But, my second batch suddenly caught a fatal disease (limberneck) and all died within a few days. Overnight, there I was, completely bankrupt and in debt up to my ears."*

In the Service

1952

According to Shelby, "*The first race I entered was held at a small airport near Caddo Mills, Texas. Quite a crowd turned out because it was one of the early Sports Car Club of America races. The course was laid out close to this little town about 40 miles from Dallas. It was a one-day affair on May 3, 1952. As far as Ed Wilkins' MG TC was concerned, it was really as stock as the day it left the factory. I can't remember much about the race except that I won.*"

His first time out, Shelby won the MG Race and the Production Race at Caddo Mills in Ed Wilkins' TC on May 3, 1952.

"The next race I entered was in August 1952 at Elkhart Lake, Wisconsin. That time, I drove an XK-120 and beat a bunch of other Jaguars to win without too much trouble."

Shelby drove Roy Cherryhomes' Cadillac-Allard J2X at Eagle Mountain, Texas, on October 26, 1952.

Jeanne Shelby is standing next to Carroll.

Shelby was in two races at Turner Air Force Base in which he finished 4th and 12th.

1952

Shelby is wondering just how he came in 1st in Charles Brown's Cad-Allard at Caddo Mills, Texas, in November 1952.

Shelby remembered the Caddo Mills event, *"It happened to be the very first race that Masten Gregory ever drove in. And, I must say, he had an awful lot of guts, cutting his teeth as a race driver in a Cadillac-powered Allard."* Gregory went on to become a leading driver of the 1950s.

1952

1953

Shelby remembered, "I won the first race I ran for Roy Cherryhomes. It was at Eagle Mountain, Texas, on October 26, 1952. The understanding I had with him was that I would drive strictly for expenses, but even so, I was pretty much thrilled. In the Southwest, good rides were mighty hard to come by in the sports car field, especially then. Suddenly, there I was with the latest equipment, a car I knew well, and a competent mechanic. Another reason I got a big charge out of the ride was that, by then, Masten Gregory was winning just about everything in our part of the country. Well, I thought, maybe we can put a stop to that, always in a friendly way, of course."

"I raced my friend Tom Graip's MG TC at Bergstrom Air Force Base near Austin, Texas, on April 12, 1953."

Shelby won at Offutt Air Force Base on July 5, 1953. "*That same weekend, there was a long-distance event that required a driver change. Jack McAfee had come to Nebraska with a Ferrari 340 Mexico in pursuit of the SCCA National Championship. As chance would have it, Jack's co-driver didn't show up and he needed a teammate. Since I had won the preliminary event, Jack asked me to join him. We ended up 2nd overall.*"

1953

At the Eagle Mountain event on August 23, 1953, Shelby remembered, *"It was very hot that Saturday morning and I had been working on the farm. I was wearing my striped farm coveralls. Eventually I realized that if I were going to get in any practice, I'd have to hurry up. So I took off just the way I was. When I got in the Allard, I realized how much cooler the coveralls were than the regular driver outfits. Well, seems like everyone got a big laugh out of that and my picture appeared in the papers. I got more publicity because of those doggone coveralls than I did for winning the race."*

Shelby raced Roy Cherryhomes' Allard five times in 1953, taking four 1sts and one 2nd. Jeanne gave him a kiss.

1953

Riddell Gregory had this to say about Carroll Shelby (recorded on July 24, 2006): "The only time I was ever able to beat Shel was at an Eagle Mountain event. I was staying with Shelby at his home in Dallas, not far from Eagle Mountain. At dinner the night before the race, he told me that if we let another Allard beat either of us, we'd be in real trouble.

"I was running my C Jag and Shel was driving an Allard belonging to Roy Cherryhomes. I was always a notoriously poor starter. At the beginning, everyone went into the first corner. Shelby and a guy in another Allard were 1st and 2nd.

"When I got to the first corner, those two and several others were ahead of me. I slammed on my brakes and started to flash my lights like I was in trouble. Everybody pulled over and I went through the corner. I ended up running 3rd behind the two Allards.

"On the 10th lap, Shelby had to make a pit stop. There I was behind the other Allard. After a few more laps, I caught and passed him. So there we were, me in 1st with the Allard right behind me. I came up on Don Rose in another Allard and I was about to lap him. But since I was so far ahead, I decided I would just follow along behind Don, a nice guy, until the race ended.

"About eight laps from the end, I got a signal from the pit with 'P12' on the board, which meant that I was only 12 seconds ahead of the 2nd-place car. On the next lap, the board said, "+12 Shel," meaning Carroll was only 12 seconds behind me. I was looking so hard at the board that when I ran down into the first corner, I almost lost it. I collected myself and passed Don in the next corner.

"I decided, 'To Hell with Shelby, I'm going to drive the way I usually drive. I'm not going to get in over my head.' When the flag finally dropped, I ended up 11 seconds ahead of Shel.

"Years later, I was telling my grandson about my days of racing and that one time I beat Shelby in a race. He didn't believe it, so I asked Carroll to send my grandson a personal letter telling him that what I said was the truth. And he did; I think my grandson still has the letter."

By the end of 1953, Shelby had garnered a host of trophies, having won 12 races in two years.

The Shelby family was complete: Daughter Sharon is between Carroll and Jeanne with sons Patrick and Michael (on the right).

1953

1954

In 1954, the Automobile Club of Argentina paid to ship four cars for Americans to drive in the 1,000 km of Buenos Aires held on January 24, 1954. The Roy Cherryhomes Cad-Allard J2X was one of those selected; Carroll Shelby and Dale Duncan drove.

Shelby remembered, "It was Dale who saved the day. The Allard's fender flapped and flew off. After several flat tires, we were reduced to running without a spare. Then the engine caught fire. When Dale saw what was happening, he raised the hood and tinkered with the carburetor without a moment's hesitation, putting out the fire." Here, Duncan is getting into the car.

World Champion Juan Manuel Fangio talking it over with Shelby and Masten Gregory.

"I got a special kick out of meeting and getting to know Fangio, because every driver has his hero and he was mine."

1954

The Aston Martin team at Sebring on March 7, 1954.

1954

Shelby is in front of the third car looking down. He was teamed with Charlie Wallace. They were running with the first six overall when the rear axle broke, putting them out of the race. Still impressed with Shelby, John Wyer suggested he go to England and that there might be a place for him on the Aston team.

1954

Shelby and Dale, who was Masten's brother-in-law, finished 10th. Even so, it was the best of the Americans, so they won the Kimberly Cup. That event, Shelby said, *"was the turning point in my racing career."*

His driving attracted the attention of Aston Martin team manager John Wyer. Shelby was offered a drive for Aston Martin in the 12 Hours of Sebring.

"In April 1954, I took off for Europe, all alone. Jeanne and the kids stayed home in Dallas." As soon as he arrived in London, he went to see John Wyer at Aston Martin in Feltham. A car had been prepared (in American colors no less) for Shelby to drive at Aintree on May 29: DB3S (#95). Much to everyone's surprise, Shelby finished 2nd to Duncan Hamilton in a C-Type Jaguar. John Wyer was happy.

1954

1954

Next, it was off to France for the June 12–13 24 Hours of Le Mans. *"I must admit I was a little nervous when I first got on that Sarthe circuit of 8.2 very fast miles."* John Wyer teamed Shelby with Paul Frère in an Aston Martin DB3S. This photo was taken at Silverstone.

1954

Friends got together at the 1954 Le Mans. From left: Shelby, Gordon Wilkins, Rob Walker (hat), Gregor Grant (mustache), Stirling Moss, Peter Collins, and Roy Salvadori.

"At 1:50 am, I noticed a bad front-end shimmy had developed as I came through Arnage and then down to White House. So I pulled into the pits and told the mechanics about it. Wyer had them jack up the car. The moment the front end was off the ground, a wheel fell off. This was caused by a broken spindle due to the bearing freezing." There was nothing to do but retire the car.

"The unforgettable thing about the Aston Martin was that it handled so well that you could call it a viceless automobile. It was what we call a 'neutral-steering car,' the result of very good suspension and ideal weight distribution. It was forgiving of mistakes too."

1954

Shelby finished 5th at Monza on June 27. Then it was on to Silverstone for the July 17 race. The start (shown here) was a bit chaotic. Shelby is in car #22. He came in 3rd overall. *"Looking back on 1954 with the team, I must say we had a pretty good time together."*

John Wyer always saw to it that we were well paid,
taken care of, and in bed by 9 pm.

1954

Shelby in an Aston Martin team car
(center, #22) at Silverstone on July 17, 1954.

1954

Peter Collins (second from left) won Silverstone, Roy Salvadori was 2nd, and Shelby (on the right) 3rd, all in Aston Martins.

"When I got back to the States in July 1954, I was broke. Roy Cherryhomes gave me a helping hand. He had bought a C-Type Jaguar (almost hidden behind the #1 Allard) that had been run over and pretzeled by a Greyhound bus in Illinois. Roy had it fixed so well that it turned out to be the best C-Type I ever drove. I ran it for him at Eagle Mountain on August 15."

1954

1954

"Driving Roy Cherryhomes' C-Type Jaguar, I won both the preliminary race and the main event at the Eagle Mountain Lake Course at the National Guard base near Fort Worth, Texas, on August 15, 1954."

Donald Healey asked Shelby to drive at Bonneville. He set a new Class D Production record in an Austin Healey.

46

1954

Shelby's time at Bonneville led Donald Healey to ask Carroll to drive in the Carrera Panamericana, the Mexican Road Race, which started on November 18, 1954. One of the most difficult and demanding races in the world, the route covered 1,932 miles from the south of Mexico at Tuxtla Gutiérrez to the north at Ciudad Juarez. This photo by *Motor Trend* photographer Bob D'Olivo shows Shelby at the start with officials and crew.

1954

"I was teamed with Roy Jackson-Moore (in the dark sport jacket in the middle). The first leg was from Tuxtla Gutiérrez to Oaxaca. I drove halfway and Roy the other. But neither of us liked being a passenger. From then on, we decided to drive alone and switch off." This photo shows Shelby about to leave Oaxaca.

1954

"When I left Oaxaca, I started dicing with those big Lincolns, really giving them hell. I passed all of them except Ray Crawford. I had just passed Vukovich and was taking off after Ray when I came around a corner a little too fast. Suddenly there was a big rock standing in my way. The rock never batted an eyelash. I went end over end four or five times like the daring young man on the flying trapeze. Only it was a lot more painful. The 175th-kilometer stone is just north of Oaxaca. The wheels on the driver's side were torn off, as was the passenger-side door. It was lucky we decided to drive solo, because if Roy had been in the passenger seat, he would probably have been killed."

1954

Shelby was seriously injured with contusions,
broken bones, and a shattered elbow along with
many cuts and bruises. He had to wait for the
ambulance for more than 6 hours until the road
reopened. He was taken to a hospital in Puebla.

1954

"Let me tell you a little something about the nurses in Mexico, at least at that time in Puebla. It seems that they came from wealthy families and only the loveliest women were allowed to take training and work in hospitals. Anyway, we were in that hospital for about 3 hours.

"While they bandaged poor Hammenich and took care of his burns, they also set my arm. The doctor told me that I should go back to Texas without delay and have my arm put in a cast because it was badly broken with the elbow knocked off. He said I should find a really good orthopedic guy as soon as possible.

"When we got to Mexico City, I found out that I couldn't leave the country. It seems that I had signed for the car we drove and I had to wait for it before they would let me out. This foolishness went on for a whole week. Some of the locals had taken a couple of the wheels as souvenirs. The Mexican law required that the same number of wheels and tires had to be taken out that were brought in. Nothing that either the U.S. or British embassies could do had any effect. So there I was, stuck in Mexico City. They wouldn't even let me post a bond for the two wheels. It's a wonder those officials didn't count the number of pieces of broken glass or the rollers in the wheel bearings.

"I was put up in a Swiss hotel that had some beautiful gardens, the name of which escapes me. During my week there, I ran into a couple of nurses from Minneapolis who knew who I was. It seemed that some friendly Mexicans had told them about my plight, that I was hurt, and needed help, so they came and took care of me. Finally, a Mexican friend appeared with two Austin Healey wheels with tires, which he claimed were the missing ones. 'We finally found them in some scrub, way down the mountain! Wasn't that lucky?'

"The officials agreed that it was indeed lucky, nodded wisely, pushed some rubber stamps on inkpads, and let me go. I finally got to the border at Juarez where you could drink uncontaminated ice water at the airport restaurant and eat all the salad you wanted. Then it was back home to Dallas.

"As soon as I got there, my doctor went to work, putting my shattered elbow in a cast and setting everything shipshape.

"'Elbows are bad things to break,' he said, 'You could lose the proper use of your arm if you had waited longer. Then where would you be as a race driver?'

"It took eight months of operations to get my arm into proper working shape again. It wasn't until August 1955 that everything finally healed and I could get rid of the cast for good."

1954

1955

Shelby and his co-driver, Phil Hill, drove Alan Guiberson's new 3-liter 750 Monza Ferrari (left) at the 12 Hours of Sebring on March 13, 1955. *"For most of the 12 hours, Phil and I diced with Mike Hawthorn and Phil Walters in their factory D-Type Jaguar."*

Eventually, the Hawthorn/Walters D-Type pulled ahead of the Shelby/Hill Ferrari. But then, mechanical problems forced the Jaguar into the pits. This allowed the Shelby/Hill car into the lead; they took the flag and were announced the winners. However, a protest was lodged and the Jaguar was declared the winner. Ferrari protested, but, after a week, the decision was upheld. Shelby and Hill were scored 2nd.

In 1955, Shelby drove in four SCCA main events for Alan Guiberson in Alan's 4.5 Ferrari 375 MM. The first was at Fort Pierce, Florida, where he managed an overall 2nd.

1955

1955

Shelby drove his last race for Alan Guiberson at an SCCA National at Torrey Pines on July 10, 1955. *"This was my first in California. I pulled ahead after the third lap and was never challenged. A duel between Shelby and Phil Hill pleased the crowd, even though Phil was a lap down."*

More than 20,000 spectators saw Shelby win the main event, the San Diego Trophy, at Torrey Pines on July 10, 1955.

After his win at Torrey Pines, Shelby met Tony Parravano (left) and his mechanic, Joe Landaker. Parravano was a contractor building houses and making millions, much of which he spent on Ferraris. Tony said to Shelby, "I would like you to drive a Ferrari for me. Any of them, take your pick. We'll start with one race. After that, we'll talk. Okay?"

1955

That one event was the Seattle Seafair held at Bremerton, Washington on July 31, 1955.

"The car Tony entered for me was a 4.9 Ferrari 375+.
It had a long wheelbase and loads of power."

The lineup included Tom Carstens in his Cadillac-Allard (left), Phil Hill in George Tilp's 3-liter Monza Ferrari (center), and Shelby (right). Also present were Ken Miles in Alan Guiberson's 375 Mexico Ferrari and John Von Neumann in his 550 Porsche Spyder.

1955

Two races were held that day in Bremerton. The first was a Seafair Preliminary that Shelby won. Then came the main event, the Seafair Trophy Race. *"When the race started, Phil Hill took the lead with me close behind. On the third lap, I passed Phil, but he stayed right on my tail for the rest of the race."* When Shelby took the flag, Hill was 7 seconds behind. Ken Miles was 3rd and John Von Neumann 4th.

1955

Pleased with the Seafair results, Parravano
asked Shelby to accompany him to
Italy where Tony intended to buy more
cars. While there, Shelby tested Ferraris
and Maseratis for Tony at the Modena
Aeroautodromo.

1955

While Shelby was in Europe, Hushke von Hanstein asked him to drive a Porsche in the Tourist Trophy that took place on September 17, 1955. The course, called the Dunrod Circuit, consisted of open roads in Northern Ireland.

"In this picture,
I am in front in car #28."

1955

"I was teamed with Masten Gregory for the 1955 Tourist Trophy. We finished 9th overall and 1st in class."

On October 16, 1955, Carroll Shelby and Gino Munaron co-drove Tony Parravano's 3-liter Monza Ferrari in the Targa Florio. *"The Targa was the hardest circuit of all to learn as well as the most difficult to go fast on."* In practice, Shelby drove the course seven times, covering a total of about 4,000 miles. When the race started, Shelby led and was running 5th overall when he stopped for a driver change. When Munaron took over, he crashed and they were out of the race.

1955

1955

Before leaving Italy, Shelby accepted a factory ride in a 250F Maserati for the October 23, 1955, Syracuse Grand Prix. It was his first time in a Formula 1 car. He placed 6th overall, which was a good showing. This photo is of the Maserati team pits.

Masten Gregory (left), Tony Parravano (center), and Carroll Shelby (right) at the December 3, 1955, race at Palm Springs. On the first lap of the main event Shelby crashed the 4.9 Ferrari, but Gregory went on to win in Tony's 3-liter Maserati. *"For years, Masten was my closest friend in racing. He had all the guts in the world. I deeply appreciated his way of showing friendship. He was soft-spoken and very gentlemanly. I thought no end of him."*

1955

1956

The first race of the 1956 season was at Palm Springs on February 26. Shelby was still with the Tony Parravano team. As it turned out, this was his last race with Parravano, who was having tax problems with Uncle Sam. It was rumored that he fled to Mexico in 1957. *"At Palm Springs, I competed in both the under–1,500-cc semi-main and the over–1,500-cc main event."* In the under, Shelby drove a 150S Maserati but failed to finish. He led every lap in the main and, as depicted here, won in a Ferrari 410 Speciale.

Aston Martin selected Carroll Shelby to drive at the 1956
12 Hours of Sebring on March 24. John Wyer teamed Shelby
with Roy Salvadori. Stirling Moss and Peter Collins, plus
Reg Parnell and Tony Brooks, were also in Astons.

1956

Shelby makes a pit stop at the 1956 Sebring. Carroll and Roy Salvadori finished 4th overall and 1st in Class D. The other two Astons failed to finish. Juan Manuel Fangio and Eugenio Castellotti won in a 3.5-liter Ferrari. Luigi Musso and Harry Schell were 2nd in another Ferrari followed by Bob Sweikert and Jack Ensley in a D-Type Jaguar. Shelby and Salvadori were eight laps behind the winner at the end.

Shelby was in the 1956 Pebble Beach races that took place on April 21–22. *"Dick Hall entered me in a 3.5-liter Monza Ferrari. At that time, Dick and I were partners in a dealership in Dallas, Texas, called Carroll Shelby Sports Cars."*

1956

On the first lap, Shelby followed Phil Hill, who was driving a 3.5-liter 860 Ferrari (#2) that had just won at Sebring.

"Phil's car didn't seem to be handling very well, so I (#24) was able to pass during the second lap and went on to win."

Ernie McAfee drove Bill Doheny's 4.4 Ferrari at the 1956 Pebble Beach. By the 26th lap, Shelby was leading, followed by Phil Hill, Jack McAfee (both in Ferraris), and Ernie McAfee. Ernie left the road near Turn 6; the car struck a tree, killing him instantly. The race ended in that order: Shelby, Hill, and Jack McAfee. It also ended racing at Pebble Beach itself. By November 1957, the course at Laguna Seca was opened and racing in Monterey has continued there ever since.

1956

Shelby is shown here leading Rod Carveth's Aston Martin DB3S at the 1956 Pebble Beach.

"I have always been very proud of my win there, particularly since it turned out to be the last one on the road course. It was one of the highlights of my race-driving years. I was fortunate to win that race because it was a tremendous boost for me as far as securing rides."

1956

Shelby drove the 750 Monza Ferrari entered by Dick Hall for the second (and last) time at Dodge City, Kansas, on April 29, 1956. He won 1st overall, adding to his points with the SCCA National Championship. The car was actually owned by Carroll Shelby Sports Cars (owned by Shelby and Hall). The SCCA rules regarding amateurism wouldn't let a company participate in their simon-pure events.

This photo was taken at Pebble Beach.

"I drove an Alfa Romeo Veloce for Max Hoffman at Cumberland, Maryland, on May 20, 1956. Actually, while the car was Hoffman's, who was the U.S. importer at the time, John Edgar had borrowed the car from Max and was the entrant.

"Ed Hugus and a few others were in similar cars. Compared to the Alfa Romeo Guiletta Spyders, those Veloces were pretty hot for their day. They had special cams, two double-throat Webers and different gearing. They went quite well except for the gearbox, which was a piece of junk. Eventually, they went to the balk-ring-type synchromesh designed by Porsche. At that time Alfa had not made a sufficient number of Veloces, so the good old SCCA classified them as 'modified,' which meant that we had to run against Lotuses and the like, which was a ridiculous situation. The best I could do was 5th overall in the under–1,500-cc main event."

In this photograph, Shelby is following Charlie Wallace (#288). Before the end, however, Shelby passed Wallace to end up 5th and Wallace finished 6th.

(Photo courtesy of the Joel Finn Collection)

1956

John Edgar (left) with Shelby.

"*My association with John Edgar began at that event. After the race he came up to me and said, 'Son, how would you like to drive for me?'*

"*Being the mercenary cash-and-carry type, I replied, 'I'd like it fine, but what's in it for me?'*

"*'What do you want?' He said, 'You name it. I'll buy you any kind of car you want.'*

"*These are sweet words for any driver to hear. But I tried not to let it go to my head. I did some fast thinking and, as a result, we had a little set-to with Luigi Chinetti and ordered the 4.9 Ferrari that was being built for that great master, Juan Fangio, to drive in Argentina. (For some reason, he never did.) It was probably the best 4.9 ever built, but that's not saying an awful lot.*

"*As it happened, when John ordered the car, it wasn't finished yet. So Chinetti lent us a 4.4 Ferrari. I won the main event at Road America on June 24 and again at Beverly, Massachusetts, on July 8. Then, Edgar borrowed a Chinetti single-seater and I set a record and won the Giant's Despair Hillclimb at Wilkes-Barre, Pennsylvania.*"

1956

"I won the June 15, 1956, Hillclimb at Mount Washington,
New Hampshire, and repeated at the Giant's Despair Hillclimb
on July 20 in Luigi Chinetti's Formula 1 Ferrari."

John Edgar actually leased the car.

1956

John Edgar again leased a 4.4 Ferrari from Chinetti and
entered Shelby at Road America on June 24, 1956.

Here, Shelby (#144) is about to pass Masten Gregory
in a 750 Ferrari Monza.

Shelby won; Lou Brero took 2nd in a D-Type Jaguar.

The Brynfan Tyddyn road races were held the same weekend as the Giant's Despair Hillclimb. Shelby drove John Edgar's 500 TR Ferrari (#128) on July 21, 1956. At left is Rob Goldich in a Ferrari Mondial. Jack McAfee is behind Shelby in John Edgar's Porsche Spyder.

"After winning Giant's Despair in a Formula 1 Ferrari, I won the main event at Brynfan Tydden the next day in Edgar's 500 TR Ferrari."

1956

On August 16, 1956, John Edgar entered Shelby, who won Bremerton, Washington's Seattle Seafair in a 4.9 Ferrari 410S.

This photo, from the Vince Howlett collection, was taken just after the start. Bill Pollack (#14) is in Tom Carstens' HMW-Chevy with Shelby to Bill's right (#98). The row in back of Shelby is Lew Florence in a Kurtis (left), Masten Gregory (center), and Jim Fox in a Jaguar Special (right).

1956

"A week after winning the Seafair, I went
to Utah to join the Austin Healey record-
attempt team on the Bonneville Salt Flats."

From left to right: unknown, Bill Pringle (Gough Industries mechanic), George Williams (representing Castrol Oil), Captain George Eyston, Carroll Shelby (hat), Gordon Whitby (Gough Industries mechanic), Roger Menadue (Austin Healey chief engineer), Roy Jackson-Moore (Shelby's co-driver), Greg Vale (Austin Healey mechanic), and Geoffrey Healey (Donald's son).

1956

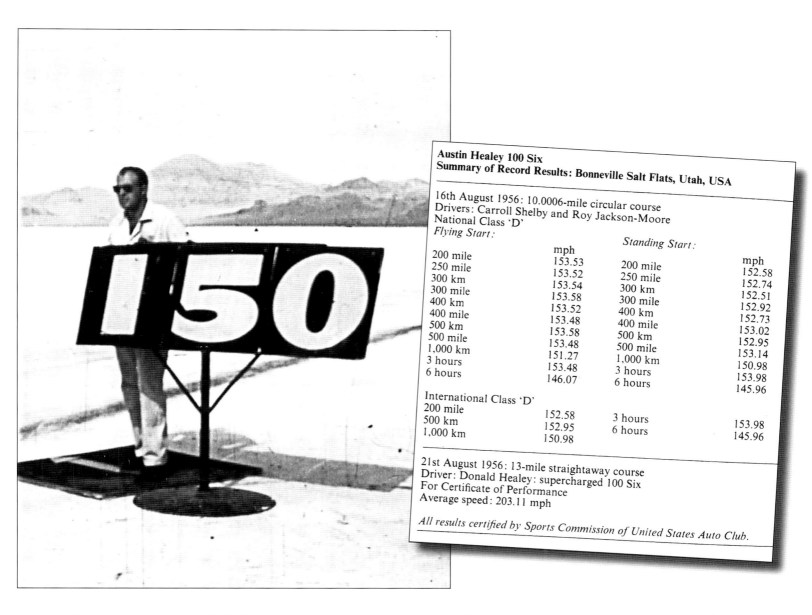

Austin Healey 100 Six
Summary of Record Results: Bonneville Salt Flats, Utah, USA

16th August 1956: 10.0006-mile circular course
Drivers: Carroll Shelby and Roy Jackson-Moore
National Class 'D'

Flying Start:	mph	Standing Start:	mph
200 mile	153.53	200 mile	152.58
250 mile	153.52	250 mile	152.74
300 km	153.54	300 km	152.51
300 mile	153.58	300 mile	152.92
400 km	153.52	400 km	152.73
400 mile	153.48	400 mile	153.02
500 km	153.58	500 km	152.95
500 mile	153.48	500 mile	153.14
1,000 km	151.27	1,000 km	150.98
3 hours	153.48	3 hours	153.98
6 hours	146.07	6 hours	145.96

International Class 'D'	mph		mph
200 mile	152.58	3 hours	153.98
500 km	152.95	6 hours	145.96
1,000 km	150.98		

21st August 1956: 13-mile straightaway course
Driver: Donald Healey: supercharged 100 Six
For Certificate of Performance
Average speed: 203.11 mph

All results certified by Sports Commission of United States Auto Club.

Gordon Whitby signals Carroll Shelby during a record run at Bonneville on August 21, 1956. At that time, Whitby was employed at Gough Industries, importer of Austin Healey cars. Whitby remembered, "Carroll was one of the most friendly race-car drivers I had ever met. When not listening to Captain Eyston's experience in driving for hours on end on the slippery salt surface, Carroll wanted to have fun and played ball with the mechanics. Seated in a race car, however, he became very serious when looking over the instruments and listening to Eyston or Geoffrey Healey's final instructions. He had an outstanding knowledge of what makes up a winning race car."

1956

Shelby (#141) started on the pole in John Edgar's 3.5-liter Ferrari 857S at the August 18, 1956 SCCA National race at the Montgomery Airport in New York.

"I won the preliminary and then went on to finish 1st overall in the main event ahead of Bill Lloyd's Maserati and three D-Type Jaguars driven by Sherwood Johnson, John Gordon Bennett, and Briggs Cunningham."

1956

On September 3, 1956, at Thompson, Connecticut, Shelby drove Edgar's 857S Ferrari into a sand bank on the first lap and then again after he had worked his way up to 2nd. He was a DNF; his brakes failed and he even lost his signature coveralls.

1956

Carroll Shelby (left) with Jim Kimberly (center) and Bob Ballinger (right). (The wives of Ballinger, Masten Gregory, and Dale Duncan were sisters.) Over the weekend of September 8 and 9, 1956, the Chicago Region of the SCCA staged two "owner-driver" races at Road America near Elkhart Lake, Wisconsin. This meant that one of the drivers had to be the actual owner of the car.

On Saturday, September 8, the event was 4 hours long; on Sunday, September 9, it was 6 hours. Jim Kimberly entered his 1,500-cc Osca MT4 with Carroll Shelby as the co-driver. They won the Saturday 4-hour race with an average speed of 74.436 mph for the 300 miles. Shelby drove 44 of the 75 laps. Kimberly's original idea was to drive his 4.4 Ferrari with Shelby on Sunday, but it turned out that the car's crankshaft was damaged. Therefore, they went out in the Osca, but had to retire with a mechanical problem.

John Kilborn and Howard Hively, in John's 4.5 Ferrari, were 1st. John Fitch and Briggs Cunningham's D-Type Jaguar finished 2nd.

The Los Angeles Region staged an SCCA National at Palm Springs on November 4, 1956. Carroll Shelby (left) is with his friend Jack McAfee. Shelby drove #98 in the race, a Ferrari 410S, but Jack drove a Ferrari 857S (not shown). They posed for photographs to publicize the race and for the program cover.

1956

1956

"I led from the start in John Edgar's 4.9 Ferrari 410S (#98) at the November 4, 1956, SCCA National at Palm Springs." Phil Hill, in a 3.5 Ferrari, is obscured behind Shelby. Bill Murphy (#6) in his Buick-Kurtis is on the left with Max Balchowsky in *Ole Yeller* behind Bill.

1956

Soon, the race developed into an intense duel between Shelby (right) and Hill. The two were never more than fractions of a second apart. They had the crowd of more than 30,000 spectators standing.

After an hour and a half of intense racing,
Starter Al Torres dropped the checkered flag
on Shelby with Hill still close behind.

1956

1956

John Edgar entered Shelby, driving the 4.9 Ferrari, in the December 1956 Nassau Speed Week. Shelby won the 100-mile Governor's Cup. *"God only knows how many times Portago (Marquis de Portago in a 3.5 Ferrari) and I bumped into each other or how many other cars we hit. I finally beat him across the finish line by about 20 feet. I think I'm proudest to have won this race except for Le Mans."*

1956

The lineup for the Governor's Trophy race, from right to left: Ray Crawford's Corvette (#117), Carroll Shelby in the Edgar 4.9 Ferrari (#98), Dr. Dick Thompson's Corvette (#15) and Jim Jefford's Corvette (#36).

1956 Nassau Speed Week winners behind the trophy table, left to right: Carroll Shelby, Stirling and Mrs. Moss, Phil Hill.

1956

Percy Knaith presented Carroll Shelby with the *Sports Illustrated* Driver of the Year trophy with Alec Ulman looking on.

"I won the SCCA National Championship that year."

1956

1957

John Edgar entered Shelby in the 4.9 Ferrari 410S (the car on the left) at Pomona, California, on January 20, 1957.

"During the 'consolation' race at Pomona on January 20, 1957, it rained cats and dogs. I (#98) *hit a hay bale and failed to finish.*" Phil Hill (#2), soaking wet, quit in disgust.

1957

1957

"In 1957, Jim Hall's brother, Dave, and I opened a business in Dallas. Jim (opposite page, right) joined us later. We became dealers, as well as distributors for a number of makes, as well as Firestone tires."

1957

After Pomona, the Edgar Equipé, along with Shelby, traveled to the East Coast to compete in the National Sports Car Day Races that were touted as the climax of the Daytona Beach Speedweeks. Bill France Sr. organized the event and NASCAR sanctioned it. George Cary was appointed as the coordinator. The SCCA announced that its members could compete providing they received no money.

The new Smyrna Beach Airport course was 2.4 miles. Shelby was mounted in the 4.9-liter 410S Ferrari in which he had been so successful the previous year and so was favored to win. But it didn't necessarily look like it was going to be easy. Tony Parravano brought another 4.9 Ferrari for Richie Ginther; Chuck Daigh was in a supercharged fuel-injected Thunderbird special. Before the start, Parravano switched Ginther to a 3-liter Ferrari and put Eric Hauser in the 4.9. Before the main event, there was a 12-lap "preliminary."

1957

Facing page, Bill France Jr. greets Shelby. Below, Shelby was the winner; here with Jan Harrison at his side.

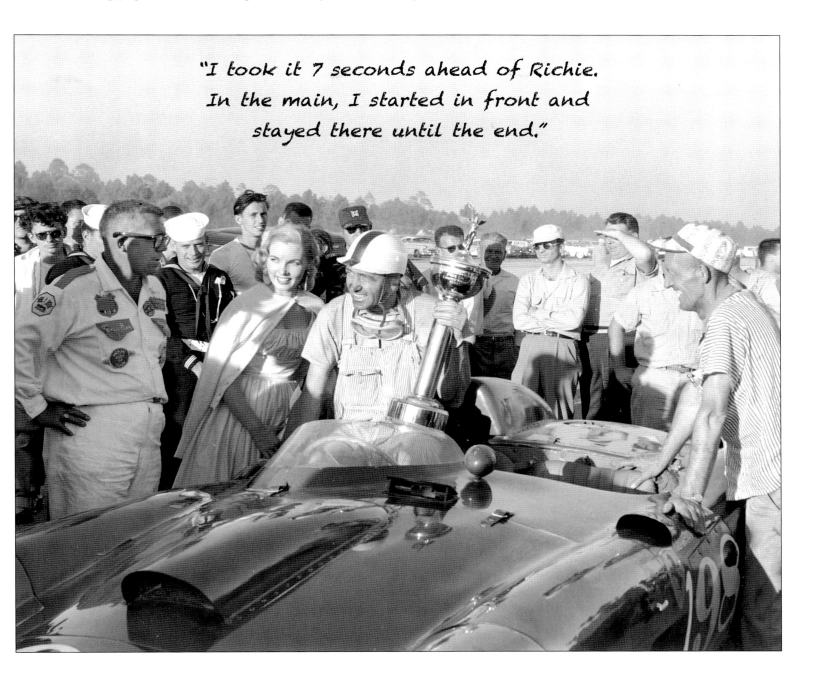

"I took it 7 seconds ahead of Richie.
In the main, I started in front and
stayed there until the end."

1957

Shelby entered the 1957 Grand Prix of Cuba (for sports cars) on February 25, driving the John Edgar 4.9 Ferrari 410S. *"I jumped into the lead at the start."*

Toward the end, while still leading, he noticed that the oil temperature was too high, so he slowed down to ensure finishing. Fangio passed and won; Shelby took 2nd.

1957

On March 10, 1957, Shelby drove a 4.5 Ferrari 375 MM at an SCCA event at Mansfield, Louisiana. The car was owned and entered by Carroll's friend, A. D. Logan.

Shelby won the main event, adding to his National Championship points.

Earlier in the day, *"I drove a 1,500-cc Elva in the modified under–1,500-cc race for 'Bo' Crim. Unfortunately the car failed to finish due to mechanical problems."*

1957

"John Edgar had a really great mechanic, Joe Landaker.

In this photo, I am consulting with Landaker regarding a problem with the Edgar Ferrari at the SCCA National at the San Joaquin County Airport near Stockton, California, on March 17, 1957. By lap 16, I was about 10 lengths ahead of 2nd-place Lou Brero in a D-Type Jaguar when the Ferrari's shifting fork broke so that I couldn't get out of third gear." Shelby had to park it and take a DNF.

1957

Enzo Ferrari (left) with Alberto Ascari, one of his drivers.

In 1957, Shelby convinced John Edgar to change from running Ferraris to Maseratis. *"For reasons that will become apparent, I made a deal for the Edgar stable to run Maseratis instead of Ferraris. Here's what happened: There had been some talk of me joining the Ferrari team in 1957. When I tried to talk turkey with il Commendatore and asked about financial arrangements, Signor Ferrari replied, 'My dear young man, you're at the beginning of your career and you should feel honored to drive for me. What's this bit about money?'*

"John Edgar was having to pay Ferrari cash on the barrelhead at strictly retail prices while, at the same time, we were winning races in Ferrari. I suggested to John that Maserati might be a bit more receptive. And sure enough, they were. The Orsi people, who had bought out the Maserati brothers some years before, tried to be cooperative.

"We got a new 3-liter and a 4.5 that had gobs of power. We also made a deal for me to drive with the Maserati team at Sebring. With the new cars, we started preparing for the rest of the major SCCA races that season. As it turned out, we won practically everything that came our way."

1957

In 1937, the Maserati brothers sold their company to the Orsi family, who ran it until 1968. Because Shelby had put together the deal between John Edgar and the Orsis, Carroll was asked to join the factory team for the 1957 12 Hours of Sebring held on March 23.

The team consisted of four cars: one 450S and three 250Ss. Juan Manuel Fangio and Jean Behra drove the 450S along with Stirling Moss/Harry Schell, Roy Salvadori/Carroll Shelby, and Ludovico Scarfiotti/Jo Bonnier in the 250Ss.

Fangio and Behra won overall with Moss and Schell 2nd. Shelby and Salvadori finished 3rd, but were disqualified because of an infringement of the refueling rules, so they were scored with a DNF.

Here, Shelby is driving a Maserati 300S.

1957

This is the front row for the start of an SCCA Regional event at Palm Springs on April 7, 1957. Shelby is in John Edgar's 300S Maserati. Next to Shel is Bob Drake in a Monza Ferrari and then Phil Hill in 121LM Ferrari. Tony Parravano owned and entered both Ferraris.

The 1957 Maserati team for Sebring was, left to right:
Harry Schell, Stirling Moss, Roy Salvadori, Juan Manuel
Fangio, Giorgio Scarlatti (in glasses behind Fangio),
Carroll Shelby, and Jean Behra.

1957

Here, Shelby is in the Edgar Maserati passing Bill Murphy in his Kurtis-Buick during a five-lap race on April 6 at Palm Springs. *"Murphy and I were lifelong friends and later partners in a dealership in the San Fernando Valley, Murphy-Shelby Dodge."*

Shelby won that preliminary event and was kissed by Race Queen Jan Harrison, a budding cinema starlet. Carroll and Jan were married in 1960.

1957

The main event at the April 7, 1957, Palm Springs race was a duel between Carroll Shelby in John Edgar's Maserati and Phil Hill in Tony Parravano's 4.4-liter Ferrari. Here, Tony (in the striped shirt) is leaning over and looking at the Ferrari engine.

Hill won over Shelby by 49 seconds. But, it was not as great a victory as it may have seemed to the 12,000 sun-drenched spectators.

During May 1957, Shelby's Texas buddy, Ebb Rose, had Carroll drive this production Corvette.

He was 3rd on May 5 at an SCCA National preliminary event at Hammond, Louisiana; he placed 2nd in the main event. On May 19, at Cumberland, Maryland, he was 2nd behind Dr. Dick Thompson in another Corvette. Dick won the 1957 SCCA National Championship.

1957

"After placing 2nd at the May 19, 1957, Cumberland Production-Car Race in Ebb Rose's Corvette, I jumped right out and into John Edgar's 300S Maserati for the next race, the main event." The race started out as a duel between Shelby and John Fitch in a Cunningham D-Type Jaguar. But on the 30th lap, John's brakes faded and he took an escape road, which allowed Shelby to take the lead and the checkered flag.

1957

Only one week after Cumberland, another SCCA National was held in Northern California. John Edgar and Carroll Shelby made the trip to the Cotati Airport near Santa Rosa.

"I led from the start at the May 26, 1957, event. But halfway through the 30-lap race, the clutch in the Maserati went out."

But this didn't faze Shelby, who could shift quite handily without the aid of a clutch.

1957

John Edgar entered Shelby and the 300S Maserati in an SCCA National held on June 2, 1957, at the Eagle Mountain National Guard Base near Fort Worth, Texas.

When the main event started, seven cars collided in the first corner. The Maserati was virtually totaled.

Before the main event, however, Ebb Rose had entered Shelby in a 10-lap production-car race driving the Corvette. Shelby failed to finish.

1957

On June 9, 1957, Shelby and the Edgar Equipé took the 300S Maserati to Connecticut where it won the 40-lap SCCA National main event at Lime Rock. For much of the race, Walt Hansgen, in a Cunningham D-Type Jaguar, was right behind Shelby. However, a clogged fuel injector forced a quick pit stop, which allowed Lake Underwood's Porsche Spyder and John Fitch's D-Type to get by. Even with the stop, Hansgen came in 4th followed by Bruce Kessler in a Testa Rossa Ferrari.

As an aside, one day I was discussing the Lime Rock circuit that John Fitch had designed. This particular race, some 50 years later, came into the conversation. To my amazement, Shelby remembered virtually every detail of the event. What a memory!

1957

The July 14, 1957, SCCA National at Marlboro, Maryland, was another victory for Walt Hansgen, who was nipping at Shelby's heels for the championship. *"I was forced out of the race with fuel line trouble after the first lap."* Bruce Kessler, in an XK-SS Jaguar (touring-equipped D-Type), was 2nd; Paul O'Shea was 3rd in his 300SL.

This photo shows Shelby (#38) at Marlboro with Ebbie Lunken's Testa Rossa Ferrari in the background.

1957

Shelby drove John Edgar's new 450S Maserati at the inaugural event at Virginia International Raceway on August 4, 1957. *"I seemed to be getting all of the possible power out of the car, no doubt thanks to its fine condition. It was an easy race. I won at better than 78 mph for the 64-mile grind. At the start, I found myself in the second row. There were two Jaguars ahead of me driven by Walt Hansgen and Charlie Wallace. But neither stayed ahead for very long. I went through the first turn with a small but clear lead. It was enough for me to stay ahead and get the checker."*

Shown here, Starter Jesse Coleman (left) and Edgar mechanic Joe Landaker are congratulating Shelby for his win.

On September 1, 1957, an SCCA race was held at Mansfield, Louisiana. Shelby's friend, A. D. Logan, entered two Ferraris: a 750 Monza and a Testa Rossa (TRC). In the preliminary event, Ray Jones drove the Monza and Bill Jankowsky drove the TRC. Just before the main event, Carroll Shelby showed up in street clothes. He borrowed a helmet and jumped into the Logan Monza, giving his name as "Jim Shelby Smith." *"I led the entire race until the very last lap when I pulled into the pits, which allowed Ray Jones, in another Logan Monza, to win."*

1957

Riverside International Raceway held its inaugural event on the weekend of September 21–22, 1957. The California Sports Car Club, which was then independent from the SCCA, organized it. On the very first lap of practice, Shelby crashed the 450S Maserati into the bank on Turn 6. He sustained severe injuries to his face. Luckily, a plastic surgeon was on duty at the Riverside Hospital and did a wonderful job.

1957

In this photo, Jackie Ginther is kissing her husband, Richie, after his win. Gerry and John Edgar are looking on with Starter Arnie Kane who is holding the flag.

1957

On November 2–3, 1957, an SCCA National was held at Palm Springs. *"I ran away with Saturday's over–1,500-cc modified and Sunday's main event."* John Edgar's 4.5-liter 450S Maserati (that Shelby had crashed at the previous month's Riverside) was repaired. When Shel came by Start/Finish to complete the first lap, there was a dent on the tail of the Maserati. Shelby and Max Balchowsky, in his *Ole Yeller*, had a little shunt in Turn 3.

And oh yes, beautiful Jan Harrison was the race queen and trophy girl, so Shelby got another kiss, with many more to follow.

1957

Carroll Shelby, in the John Edgar 450S Maserati (#98),
has just passed Walt Hansgen, in the Briggs Cunningham
D-Type Jaguar, in Turn 6 at Riverside on November 17, 1957.

1957

In 1957, it occurred to Shelby and Jim Hall that a Lister would accommodate a small-block American V-8. *"We went to England, met with Brian Lister, and came home with six rollers. Our idea was for Carroll Shelby Sports Cars to become the U.S. Lister distributor."* Shelby and Hall sold five but installed a 283-ci Chevrolet engine in one that Hall raced. The idea failed to progress because Lister essentially went out of business. The experience, however, gave Shelby an introduction for putting an American V-8 into a British chassis.

Here, Jim Hall is in the Lister Chevrolet at the *Examiner* Grand Prix at Pomona on March 8, 1959.

1957

The last and most important race of the Bahamas Speed Week was the Nassau Trophy on December 7. Stirling Moss (left) won in a 3.5 Ferrari followed by Shelby (center) in the Maserati and Phil Hill in a 4.1 Ferrari (right). Nassau chairman "Red" Crise is behind them.

In those days, the last big event of the season was the Bahamas Speed Week at Nassau. John Edgar entered Shelby in the 450S Maserati in 1957.

1957

1958

The photograph above shows Phil Hill (#8) about to pass C. Perdisa (#26) in a 3-liter Maserati along Havana's main street, the Malecón. The photo on the facing page is of Carroll Shelby (left) Stirling Moss (middle), and Bruce Kessler (right).

The 1958 Grand Prix of Cuba had to be the most bizarre race ever. It was the first major event for Shelby that year. It took place on February 24 in the streets of Havana. The lineup was impressive: Juan Manuel Fangio in a 4.7 Maserati and Stirling Moss in a 4.1 Ferrari. Shelby drove John Edgar's 450S Maserati. Others included Phil Hill, Masten Gregory, Wolfgang von Trips, Porfirio Rubirosa, Paul O'Shea, and Bruce Kessler.

At that time, the dictator Fulgencio Batista governed Cuba. Meanwhile, a band of militants in Cuba's Sierra Maestra, led by Fidel Castro and his brother Raúl, were fomenting revolution. The day before the race, Fangio was abducted by one of Castro's armed men, who told him, "In the name of the 26th of July Movement, follow me." Then taken to a secret location by several kidnappers, Fangio said he was treated with courtesy. Hearing of Fangio's plight, Moss, according to Kessler, was "just going ballistic."

A huge crowd, estimated at more than 200,000, was on hand to see the start. Masten Gregory led, followed by Stirling Moss and then Shelby. Moss passed Gregory, but on the sixth lap, using what Shelby later described as "some pretty daring driving," Gregory retook the lead. But then, a Cuban amateur, Armando Cifuentes (driving a 2-liter Ferrari) went into the thickly packed crowd killing 6 or 7 spectators and injuring another 30 to 40, including himself. The race was red flagged. Gregory, followed by Moss and Shelby, drove slowly back to the Start/Finish. Just before the line, Moss sped up and passed Gregory.

Gregory protested; he and Moss agreed to split the prize money. At about 10 pm that evening, Fangio was taken to the Argentine Embassy and released. The next day, all left Havana. Almost a year later, Castro's revolution succeeded. At this writing, he and his brother remain in power.

1958

"In the March 22, 1958, Sebring 12-hour grind I drove an Aston Martin DBR1/1 for the factory team. That year, the team consisted of only two cars: Stirling Moss and Tony Brooks in one with my old partner, Roy Salvadori, and I in the other.

"Moss took an early lead, followed closely by Mike Hawthorn's new 3-liter Ferrari Testa Rossa, then Roy in our car, and Phil Hill in another Testa Rossa. Mike, Roy, and Phil were running about 5 seconds apart from one another and some 30 seconds behind Stirling. Stirling really seemed to have the bit between his teeth, consistently lapping at speeds well under the previous year's record. When the race was 2 hours old, Stirling had pushed the DBR1 at such a rate that he held a clear 2-minute lead over the rest of the field.

"Then it was my turn to take over from Roy. I'll be darned if after a few laps, the gearshift handle didn't break off! The weld broke and there was nothing to do about it. Scratch one Aston, but that still left us in the lead with the other car. Tony, despite the slow pit stop, did a great job of hanging onto 1st place and beating off a Ferrari attack. At 2:15 pm, he came in to let Moss take over again. This time, the car was in the pit for 3 minutes, 32 seconds while more tires were changed and new brake pads installed.

"Moss took off like the proverbial scalded cat, determined to close the gap that separated him from the Peter Collins' Ferrari that had taken the lead during the pit stop. Moss was only 15 seconds behind and everyone started to get excited. But that was the end of it. The Aston transmission broke, ending our 1958 Sebring effort."

1958

John Edgar entered Shelby in the 450S Maserati (#98) at the April 12–13, 1958, SCCA National at Palm Springs. He won Saturday's over–1,500-cc modified event. However, on Sunday, after a nose-to-tail duel, Dan Gurney, in Frank Arciero's 4.9 Ferrari (#69), won by a nose.

"Later, Dan Gurney and I became lifelong friends and occasional partners in various enterprises."

1958

From May through September 1958, Shelby raced in Europe for Aston Martin, the Centro Sud team, and Temple Buell. On May 18 at Spa, Belgium, he was 3rd overall in an Aston Martin DBR2. Driving a 250F Formula 1 Maserati, he failed to finish in the Grand Prix of France (shown). *"I was a member of the Scuderia Centro Sud team sponsored by Mimmo Dei, a Rome Maserati auto dealer."*

The Centro Sud team (left to right): two mechanics, Shelby, Phil Hill (not on the team), Troy Ruttman, another mechanic, team owner Mimmo Dei, and Giulio Borsari.

1958

The Tourist Trophy, run at Goodwood, was held on September 13, 1958. Shelby was part of the Aston Martin team. The company entered three DBR1s (#7, #8, and #9). The team consisted of Stirling Moss with Tony Brooks (#7), Roy Salvadori with Jack Brabham (#9), and Carroll Shelby with Stewart Lewis-Evans (#8).

In the United States, Shelby raced a 5.7-liter 450S Maserati for Temple Buell at Riverside on October 12, 1958, where he was a DNF thanks to two cylinders that failed. He ran again at Palm Springs on November 2 and won.

The Nassau Speed Week was the last major event of the 1958 season. *"I drove John Edgar's 450S Maserati in the Nassau Trophy, the week's major event. Unfortunately, the engine failed to restart after a pit stop, so I failed to finish."*

1958

The Aston Martin team scored
an outstanding victory at the
1958 Tourist Trophy, finishing
1st, 2nd, and 3rd.

1958

1959

In 1959, Carroll Shelby and Jim Hall once again dipped their toes into the constructor waters (this time with Gary Laughlin). They persuaded General Motors to sell them Corvettes without bodies. Then, they made a deal with Italian coachbuilder Sergio Scaglietti to design and build aluminum bodies and coachwork. General Motors delivered three that were sent to Italy. The result was something that looks similar to the Scaglietti-designed GT350 Ferrari. It weighs approximately 400 pounds less than a production Corvette. It was dubbed the Corvette Italia. But then, fearful that it would cut into Corvette sales, General Motors backed out of the deal, so the idea died. Shelby's Italia (shown) is currently owned by the Petersen Automotive Museum.

The first big sports-car race in the United States for the 1959 season was on March 8 at the Pomona Fairgrounds. Sponsored by the *Los Angeles Examiner*, it hosted some big-name drivers and large prize money. John Edgar entered Shelby in the 450S Maserati. In early going (shown here), Dan Gurney, in the Arciero 4.9 Ferrari (#69), led; he was followed by Max Balchowsky's *Ole Yeller* Buick Special (#70) and Shelby's Maserati (#98). The 450S dropped out with mechanical problems, as did Gurney's Ferrari. Ken Miles won in a Porsche Spyder.

It's interesting to note that Gurney and Shelby
later became partners as well as lifelong friends,
and that Shelby drove Max's *Ole Yeller* in 1960.

1959

Shelby spent much of 1959 in Europe driving for Aston Martin.

First was a Formula 1, the British Grand Prix held at Silverstone, in England, on May 2. Both Roy Salvadori and Shelby were in Astons. *"Both Roy and I were up there with Jack Brabham. He couldn't get away from us. But on the last lap, I dropped a valve, so Roy finished a close 2nd to Jack while I failed to finish."*

1959

Next, Shelby went to the Nürburgring in Germany to drive an RSK Porsche for Wolfgang Seidel. *"From the start, I led all other Porsches, but then, the engine dropped a valve, so I wasn't able to finish."* Here, he is describing the race to Seidel.

Shelby was teamed with Roy Salvadori in an Aston Martin DBR1 for the 24 Hours of Le Mans held on June 20–21, 1959. Shelby is in car #5 in 6th place just after the start.

1959

*"The high-point of my driving
career was when Roy Salvadori
and I won Le Mans in 1959." Shelby
is taking the checker in this photo.*

1959

1959

FACING PAGE: During July, August, and September 1959, Shelby drove Formula 1 Grands Prix for Centro Sud and Temple Buell. *"My best finish was a 9th at the Grand Prix of Great Britain on July 19."* The #4 was Shelby's car. He also drove a Formula 2 at Brands Hatch for Alan Brown.

"On September 3, 1959, I was back in an Aston Martin for the Tourist Trophy at Goodwood." Ferrari, Porsche, and Aston Martin were in a battle for the Manufacturers' Championship. As this was the last race of the season, the victor won the Championship.

Shelby (left) with Stirling Moss (center) and Roy Salvadori (right) won the 1959 Tourist Trophy and the Championship for Aston Martin.

1959

Shelby returned for the 1959 Nassau Speed Week. Jim Hall prepared a Maserati Birdcage for Shelby in the week's main event, the Nassau Trophy. But the car developed a serious oil leak during practice and couldn't be repaired in time. Dan Gurney was supposed to drive a Birdcage for the Camoradi Team, but he had been injured in a go-kart accident, so the ride was offered to Shelby.

"For the first half of the event, Stirling Moss, in an Aston Martin, led with me close behind in 2nd. But then the de Dion tube broke in the Maserati and I had to park it."

1959

1960

The first race of the 1960 season was the Grand Prix of Cuba on February 28. Shelby drove a Porsche RSK for Camoradi, but failed to finish. Stirling Moss (#7) led from the start and won in a Camoradi Maserati. Castro had taken power and things weren't the same in Cuba.

Next, the Camoradi team went to Sebring for the 12 Hours on March 25–26, 1960. The members (left to right: Shelby, Dan Gurney, Stirling Moss, and Masten Gregory) relaxed and talked it over.

Shelby drove a Birdcage, but it blew a gasket, so he failed to finish.

Shelby was 4th on the first lap of the 1960 *Examiner* Grand Prix at Riverside.
He's followed by Jack Brabham in a Cooper Monaco, Chuck Howard in the
Huffaker-Chevrolet Special, Lloyd Ruby in the #45 Micro-Lube Maserati 450S,
and Chuck Stevenson in the Chuck Porter Mercedes-Corvette.

1960

When Shelby won the 1960 *Examiner* Grand Prix at Riverside on April 3, he received an enthusiastic kiss from Race Queen Jan Harrison.

This was not the first time he had been kissed by Jan, nor would it be the last.

On May 1, 1960, Shelby drove an RSK Porsche for Western States Porsche distributor John Von Neumann at Vacaville, California. It was an amateur event hosted by the California Sports Car Club, which was not then affiliated with the SCCA. He was 2nd in class and 6th overall.

1960

"On June 19, 1960, I drove a DKW
Formula Junior in the Vanderbilt
Cup at the Roosevelt Raceway at
Westbury, New York." He failed
to finish. *Motor Trend* Staff
Photographer Bob D'Olivo came
from California to cover the event.

1960

The next race was the Continental Divide Grand Prix held at Castle Rock near Denver on June 27. Harry Heuer had entered the Scarab that was usually driven by Augie Pabst. Augie was at Le Mans, so Heuer gave the ride to Shelby. The Denver newspaper covered the event: "Carroll Shelby, king of the sports car drivers, got a chariot worthy of royalty, Sunday, and smashed all the Continental Divide Raceway's records before 9,283 fans. The 37-year-old racing veteran from La Mirada, California, piloted the magnificent Scarab #2 of the Meister Brauser racing team in a wire-to-wire victory in the 100.8-mile Colorado International."

1960

In pursuit of the USAC Sports Car Championship, Shelby drove Max Balchowsky's *Ole Yeller* (#10) at a July 31, 1960, race at Road America at Elkhart Lake, Wisconsin.

"I really liked Max; we got on famously."

Shelby went out with mechanical troubles while leading.

1960

Max Balchowsky had Shelby up again for the next race at Santa Barbara on September 4. Shelby must have fallen in love with the car because this was not a professional event and there was no prize money. Like most California Sports Car Club meetings, there were two main events, one on Saturday and another on Sunday. Shelby was the pre-race favorite; he led on Saturday until the bottom end of the engine blew out. Max didn't have time to fix it, so the car was a scratch on Sunday.

This photo was taken at Elkhart Lake, Wisconsin.

1960

Shelby was kissed by Jan Harrison so many times that he asked her to marry him. Jan's official filmography shows that, although she never acted in a feature motion picture, she appeared in several TV shows, including *Flipper*, *Bonanza*, *Rawhide*, *Death Valley Days*, and *Gunsmoke*. She started her TV career in 1958, appeared in more than 30 episodes, and retired from acting after the 1962 season.

1960

"In September 1960, Jan and I wanted to get married. John Edgar and his wife, Gerry, drove us to Tijuana, Mexico, in the Edgar Rolls-Royce. After watching the bullfights, we got married."

This photograph shows the group (from left): Carroll, John, Jan, and Gerry. According to Shelby, a few months later he returned to Mexico and terminated the marriage. He and Jan remained friends, however, for the rest of Shelby's life.

1960

Just back from Mexico, Shelby entered *The Los Angeles Times* Grand Prix at Riverside on October 16, 1960, in Frank Harrison's Maserati Birdcage. More than 80,000 spectators watched as Shelby qualified just behind Bill Krause's brand-new Type 61 Birdcage. Here, Shelby is leading Phil Hill's Ferrari.

Shelby was battling for 3rd in the October 16, 1960, *Times* Grand Prix when his engine went sour and he ended up finishing in 5th. Some sources have stated that this was Shelby's last race. Not true; there was one more.

1960

Shelby's last race was the Pacific Grand Prix for Sports Cars, a USAC event at Laguna Seca on October 23, 1960. He drove Frank Harrison's Maserati Birdcage (#98), seen here on the grid.

"I wanted to be sure of winning the U.S. Sports Car Championship, so to nail it down, I decided to go for some extra points."

1960

Shelby raced for the last time on October 23, 1960, at Laguna Seca. He placed 2nd overall in the Pacific Grand Prix for Sports Cars, winning the 1960 USAC Sports Car Championship. In addition, he was named Driver of the Year for the second time.

"After I was diagnosed with heart trouble, I decided to hang up my helmet and quit racing."

This was at the end of the 1960 season.

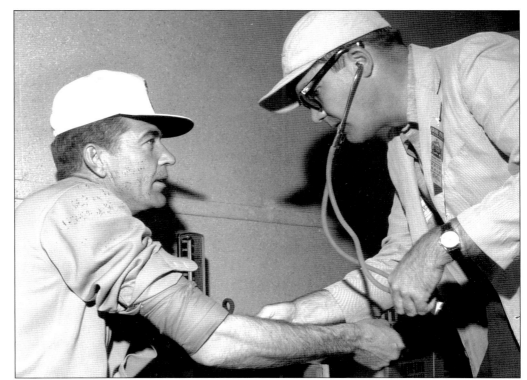

1961

Shelby is shown here (left) with two students and Pete Brock (right). Carroll hired Brock to manage the school and provide much of the instruction.

A successful sports car of the time was the British AC with a 2-liter Bristol engine. In this photo, two AC-Bristols race at Pomona on October 26, 1957. In 1961, Bristol stopped producing the engine, leaving the cars powerless. *"In September 1961, I sent a letter to AC proposing that the company produce rollers and ship them to me for the installation of an American V-8. Then, I contacted Dave Evans at Ford who had two 260-ci engines shipped to me."* AC was interested, so they sent Shelby a roller that arrived at Dean Moon's shop in Santa Fe Springs, California, where Shelby rented space.

"When the roller arrived, Dean Moon, his men, and I installed the Ford engine and a BorgWarner 4-speed transmission." They were able to accomplish this in one day! Shelby and Moon then took it for a test drive. *"Sometime later, I called it a Cobra. I seem to remember that the name came to me one night in a dream."*

1961

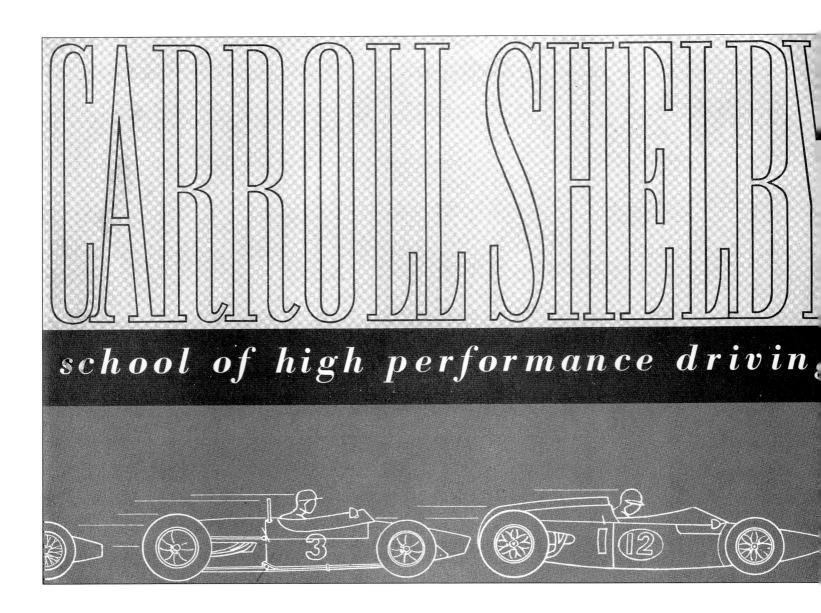

CARROLL SHELBY

school of high performance driving

"*I opened my Shelby School of High Performance Driving in 1961,
using Riverside Raceway as a schoolroom and playground.*"

1961

The course will be open to all owners and drivers of acceptable sports cars and other qualified vehicles, according to the rules and regulations stipulated on the enclosed application and inspection forms, and elsewhere within this text. The following are the general requirements for eligibility to the Carroll Shelby School of High Performance Driving.

1. Both men and women drivers are accepted.

2. Potential students must be in excellent physical condition.

3. Each enrollee must complete the course to qualify for certification by the School.

4. Minors must receive individual approval of the school management, and must have signed authorization by either parent or guardian.

Prior to the first class session, enrollment must be made to 10820 South Norwalk Boulevard, Santa Fe Springs, California. Upon enrollment, a 25% deposit is required with the balance due on the first day of class.

Individual, private instructions
using School equipment for either
beginners or advanced students...$500.00

Individual, private instruction using
student's own equipment...$250.00

Carroll Shelby School of High Performance Driving
10820 SOUTH NORWALK BOULEVARD • SANTA FE SPRINGS, CALIFORNIA
Telephone: OXbow 8-9733

The only group classes will be taught on week-ends when Riverside Raceway is available. These classes will consist of five students. The cost will be $125, and will consist of 10 hours, five hours on Saturday and five hours on Sunday.

Classes fill rapidly, so we urge you to enroll immediately if you wish to take the course in the near future.

BROCHURE DESIGNED BY RALPH STARKWEATHER

A $90 ad in the monthly magazine *Sports Car Graphic* resulted in some 1,500 requests for the brochure shown here and on the next two pages.

CARROLL SHELBY SCHOOL OF HIGH P[ERFORMANCE]

Carroll Shelby, winner of Le Mans 1959, boasts 10 years of international racing experience. After winning the USAC championship at Riverside in 1960, he retired to develop the drivers' school at Riverside International Raceway and enter into several other racing enterprises, among them distributorship for Goodyear racing tires in the 11 western states.

For a number of years European driving schools have been seriously involved in developing new talent for the raceways of the world, and more competent drivers for the highway. We have seen these schools in action off-season at Nurburgring, Brands Hatch, Finmere, Modena Autodrome and Montlhery, and were so impressed by their efforts and objectives that we decided to initiate a series of courses in high performance driving in the United States.

The Carroll Shelby School of High Performance Driving, however, is unique in that it operates on a year-round basis, and has at its

objectives

1. To instruct all categories of drivers in the science of high-speed driving.
2. To encourage safety on both the highway and raceway.
3. To provide a continuous program of driving education for sport, entertainment and competition.
4. To extend, in the future, the experience of the School to the members of Federal, State and civic groups who must drive at high speed due to their emergency functions.
5. To train championship drivers through scientific education.

school ar[e]

WORLD RENOWN RIVE[R]
The School's present site is at the located just a few miles outside of Riv[erside] California. The course, one of the fin[est in] America today, is 3.275 miles in length ideal for training and practice in t[he] incorporates varied and challenging conditions; including up and down hill esses, and over a mile straight, plus mile oval for special events.

Riverside and nearby communities excellent accommodations. We will assis[t] participants and spectators in planning itinerary and in making reservations.

SPEED ON THE RACEWAY

1961

MANCE DRIVING

osal one of the world's finest tracks along
extremely adequate classroom facilities.
student will be personally instructed in
science of competitive driving by Carroll
by, assisted by Paul O'Shea and Joe Lan-
r. Each brings with him countless hours
successful racing experience.

staff

Personal instruction will be given by Carroll Shelby
and Paul O'Shea, both former winners of the *Sports
Illustrated Driver of the Year Award*. They will be
assisted by Joe Landaker, who has been Carroll
Shelby's mechanic for 10 years, and who was selected as the *New York Times Mechanic of the Year*
in 1957.

course curriculum

Classes will be held five days a week, Monday through Friday, starting at
8 a.m. Each day two hours will be spent in the classroom, two hours on the
course, with the remainder of the afternoon for practice. Students will
receive individual instruction and supervision. Driving conditions will be
strictly controlled in the interest of maintaining a perfect safety record.

The course itself will cover proper shifting, correct cornering, basic car
maintenance and driving courtesy both on the track and the highway.

After 20 hours of instruction, graduates will receive a certificate which will
greatly aid in securing a competition license.

ocation

RNATIONAL RACEWAY

Course — 3.275 miles

equipment

The car used should be that
which the student plans on
driving upon completion of the course. In this way, the
student can gain maximum benefit from his instruction. The School will make available cars in stock,
sports and formula categories.

Below are the general requirements relating to car and equipment:
1. Each car must first pass technical inspection by an authorized facility. This can be done by track
   personnel.
2. Each car must be equipped with a roll bar which meets the School's rigid safety requirements.
3. Equipment musts are: crash helmet, gloves and safety belt (all of which may be purchased at
   the track).
4. It is suggested that each driver have fireproof clothing.

eligibility and enrollment

SAFETY ON THE HIGHWAY

1962

The prototype Cobra (CSX2000) was completed in April 1962. Shelby and a companion went for a spin. This car is still in the Shelby collection.

> "I created a new company and had it incorporated in California. I named it Shelby American."

This first PR photo was taken shortly after Dean Moon painted the prototype. Shelby is shown here with his secretary and longtime companion, Joan Sherman.

1962

The second AC roller was shipped in July 1962 to Shelby's buddy (and mine), Ed Hugus. At the time, Hugus had a large dealership in Pittsburgh, which is where a 260-ci Ford engine and transmission were installed.

Shelby appointed Ed as his first dealer and then the Eastern States distributor.

Ed drove a Cobra (#4) at Le Mans in 1963 (shown). Unfortunately, the engine failed while he was running in 4th overall.

FACING PAGE: *"I appointed Peyton Cramer (left) as the general manager of Shelby American. My new company took over the facility in Venice, California, that had previously housed Lance Reventlow's Scarab project."* Lance had given up the business; Shelby took over Lance's lease on the Princeton Drive shop (shown here) in March 1962.

1962

Meanwhile, the Shelby School of High Performance Driving continued operations at Riverside Raceway. Beginning in 1962, Cobras were used for some of the instruction.

In this photo, John Timanus (standing) talks with student John Morton. Soon thereafter, John Morton became the janitor at the Venice shop.

1962

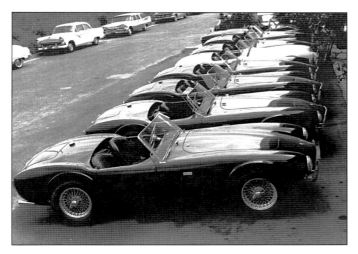

"*By August 1962, eight Cobras had been completed at my Venice shop. I submitted an application to the FIA for homologation for my cars to race with other production cars.*" The FIA requirement was that at least 100 cars had to be completed within a 12-month period. Nevertheless, the FIA approved the application and, from then on, Cobras competed as production cars.

Among his many talents, Shelby was a master at PR. "*After we completed the prototype, I talked* Sports Car Graphic *editor John Christy into testing it.*" The article appeared in the May 1962 edition. Christy called the car's acceleration "explosive." The result was that customers began to place orders.

1962

"I wanted to see if the Cobra would hold its head up in a race, so I hired Bill Krause to drive."

"The first test took place at Riverside on October 13, 1962. Its performance was impressive, but we determined that some changes were necessary. Cooling slots and scoops were added, the compression was raised, and a Spalding Flamethrower ignition was installed."

1962

As a result of the test, Shelby entered Bill Krause in a 3-hour endurance race at Riverside on October 13, 1962. Here, Shelby American Chief Mechanic Phil Remington and another mechanic, Don Pike, are kneeling, making adjustments to the driver-side front wheel.

"That's me in the background, standing with my hands on my hips and wearing sunglasses."

1962

That first race for the Cobra was also the first one for the Stingray Corvette. Top drivers Bob Bondurant and Dave MacDonald were there to drive the Corvettes. At the start, MacDonald led and was followed by Krause; soon they were swapping the lead. On the ninth lap, Dave dropped out with mechanical troubles and Krause increased his lead over the rest of the field by half a lap. Then the Cobra suffered a broken axle.

"I had my old racing number, 98, painted on the body. That race demonstrated the potentialities of my new car."

1962

The December Bahamas Speed Week was traditionally the last event of the international racing season.

"I entered Bill Krause to drive the #98 Cobra." Holman & Moody entered two Cobras, one of which was for Augie Pabst (#18). John Everly entered his own car as a private entry. Unfortunately all failed to finish due to various mechanical problems. However, Krause gave a scare to the favored Ferraris. He would have won except that he was called into his pit because of a crew miscalculation.

1963

"The most significant thing that happened to me in 1963 was that Ken Miles came to work for me at Shelby American."

Miles was an Englishman who came to the United States to work for the MG distributor. He built an MG Special (shown) that, in 1953, won every single race he entered including Pebble Beach. During the 1950s, he was the president of the California Sports Car Club that organized most of the races in Southern California. In 1956, he went to drive for the Western States Porsche/Volkswagen distributor, John Von Neumann, and began an outstanding career in racing Porsches. In 1959, Ken and his wife, Mollie, became naturalized U.S. citizens. Miles opened his own shop in North Hollywood in 1960.

"Ken soon became my most important Shelby American employee. He and I also became fast friends. Miles was the heart and soul of our testing program. He was world-class and the best test driver I ever knew. Since his death, there's not a day in my life that I don't think of Ken Miles."

In 1962, Ken Miles raced a Sunbeam Alpine (#50) for the dealer. In this photo by Allen Kuhn, Miles has just passed Davey Jordan's Porsche at Santa Barbara. Despite his great driving, the car didn't do well because it was underpowered. The manufacturer, Roots Group, was looking for a better engine. Taking notice of the Cobra, Roots contracted with Shelby to install a 260-V-8 Ford. But Shelby American had other priorities, so Miles was given a Ford engine to install at his shop. He accomplished the task over a single weekend!

1963

In the meantime, however, Miles came to work at Shelby American where the Roots contract was fulfilled in eight weeks by Shelby mechanics Ted Sutton (left) and Jim O'Leary (right). *"Roots wanted me to have the car raced, so I assigned my friend Lew Spencer* (in the car) *to drive."* The prototype was sent back to England where production started after Roots ordered a large number of Ford engines. It was ironic in that Chrysler had acquired a considerable slice of Roots, but Chrysler didn't make a suitable engine.

The new car was dubbed the Sunbeam Tiger, and a production model was sent to Shelby where Spencer campaigned it during 1963 with middling success (he only won one race).

In 1964, Roots gave the racing job to the Sports Car Forum in Columbus, Ohio, and Shelby was out of it.

1963

In 1959, Cooper Cars of England introduced a very successful sports-racing car, the Cooper Monaco. In this photo by Allen Kuhn, Sir Jack Brabham (left), in a Cooper Monaco, is dueling with Carroll Shelby, in a Birdcage Maserati, for the lead at the 1960 *Examiner* Grand Prix at Riverside on April 3.

1963

FACING PAGE: In order to compete on the world stage, Shelby needed a sports-racing car that could accommodate a small-block Ford engine. He decided on the Cooper Monaco. *"In 1963, I contacted John Cooper in England, bought two Monaco rollers, and had 289-ci Ford engines installed."* Here, Shelby (standing) talks it over with Dave MacDonald who is sitting in the first King Cobra at the Shelby American plant in Venice.

Following the testing period, Dave MacDonald won the *Times* Grand Prix at Riverside on October 13. At first, Shelby called the cars "Cooper Fords." Steve Smith, writing in *Car and Driver* magazine, thought up the name "King Cobra," and the moniker caught on.

Dave MacDonald won again at Laguna Seca on October 20, 1963.
That year's U.S. Road Racing Championship went to Shelby.

1963

At the same time, during the 1963 season, Shelby American was producing, preparing, and racing Cobras.

"Ken Miles was my lead Cobra driver for Shelby American. During 1963, he scored three 1st places and seven 2nd-place finishes, securing the Drivers' Championship for himself and the Manufacturers' Championship for my company, Shelby American."

1963

"Bob Holbert (left) and Ken Miles, in a Shelby Cobra, finished 1st in the GT Class and 2nd overall at the Road America 500 on September 8, 1963."

1963

In 1963, Shelby American Production Department Manager Leonard Parsons suggested that the company institute a drag-racing program to boost the morale of the employees.

Shelby agreed and provided a Cobra, a company pickup with trailer, and a $6,000 budget. To prepare the car, the 260-ci engine was replaced with a full-race 289 and a large Sun tachometer was installed in front of the driver. The rest was pretty much stock.

1963

By the end of 1963, Cobras were
receiving a lot of press attention.

"*Steve McQueen* (right) *came to see me one day so that he could check out one. I let him take a test drive with me in the passenger seat, but he ended up not buying one.*"

1963

1964

The Shelby American Drag-Racing Team (left to right): Tony Stoer, Jere Kirkpatrick, Randy Shaw, and Leonard Parsons. Tony set an A/SSP Class record of 12.81 seconds and 108.95 mph at Phoenix in February 1964. Then in June, he set another class record at Riverside of 12.00 seconds and 114.83 mph. Ford took notice and sent a telegram to Shelby: "You will campaign at all major NHRA and AHRA events."

It became obvious to Shelby that his Cobras needed a more aerodynamic shape in order to win at Le Mans (with its long Mulsanne Straight).

The roadsters couldn't achieve the necessary top speed, so Shelby decided to make a coupe version. The project was assigned to Pete Brock (facing the camera) who had graduated from the Art Center College of Design and worked on the Stingray design at General Motors. *"Pete began to work for me in October 1963 and finished the job in 90 days."* Ken Miles sorted it out at Riverside. Shelby credited its success as much to Miles as to Brock. The coupes were able to reach a top speed of 198 mph.

"I assigned Davey MacDonald to drive the coupe in its first race at the February 16, 1964, Daytona." Its debut was spectacular, hence its name; from then on, it was the Shelby Cobra Daytona Coupe. *"After winning at Sebring, I had Dan Gurney and Bob Bondurant drive it at Le Mans."* They finished 4th overall and 1st in the GT category. In 1965, Lew Spencer, Jim Adams, Phil Hill, Ed Leslie, Allen Grant, Bob Bondurant, and Jo Schlesser drove Daytonas at the March 12 Hours of Sebring. Bondurant and Schlesser won the GT category.

1964

"I knew that, as good as it was, the 289-ci Ford engine wasn't powerful enough. A 427-ci Ford was being used in NASCAR races, so I told Miles to stuff one into a Cobra chassis." With 100 more horsepower, Miles and Bondurant (shown) took the prototype for testing at Riverside. As a result, a number of modifications were made.

1964

"I decided to enter the 427 in the 1964 12
Hours of Sebring. I assigned Ken Miles and
John Morton, who started out as my janitor, to
drive. After leading for a time, Miles got tired
and Morton took over. Unfortunately, just
before dark the engine blew. But the car had
demonstrated its potential."

1964

The first lap of the 1964 Sebring turned out to be a wild melee. The Ken Miles/John Morton 427 Cobra (#1) is in the center of this photo with Ken driving. Even though the 427 didn't finish, the 289 Cobras scored a clean sweep in the GT category.

1964

"My good buddy Dan Gurney (in the Shelby Cobra Daytona Coupe #21) won the Grand Touring Class at the 1964 Tourist Trophy at Goodwood in England. Here, Innes Ireland is following close behind in a GTO Ferrari."

"In March 1964, I announced that my Cobras would challenge Ferrari for the World Manufacturers' Championship."

1964

The first foray was the Targa Florio on Sicily in April. The only Cobra that finished was the Dan Gurney and Jerry Grant car (shown); they took 8th.

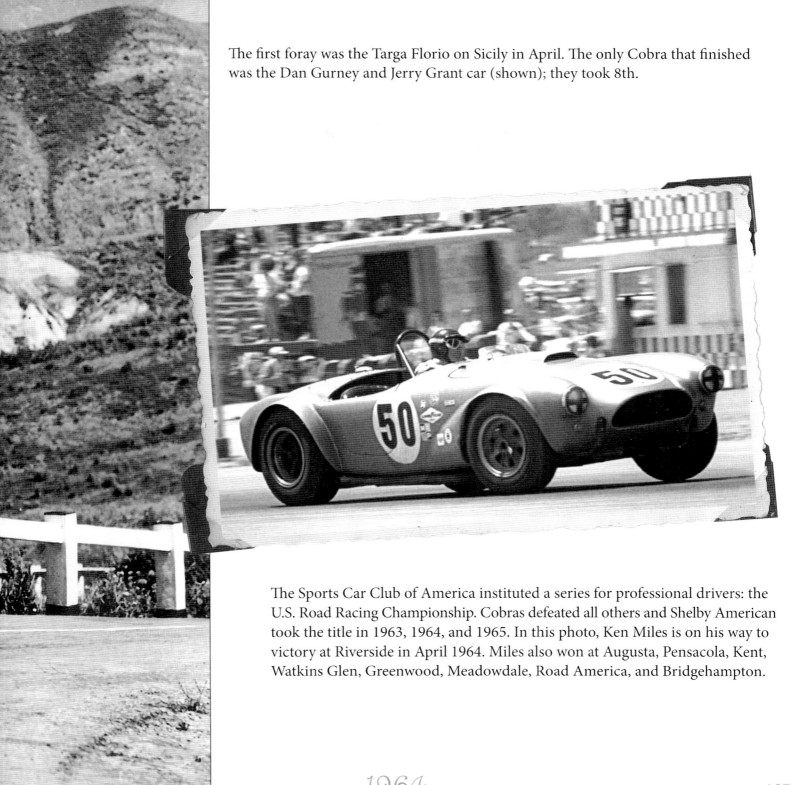

The Sports Car Club of America instituted a series for professional drivers: the U.S. Road Racing Championship. Cobras defeated all others and Shelby American took the title in 1963, 1964, and 1965. In this photo, Ken Miles is on his way to victory at Riverside in April 1964. Miles also won at Augusta, Pensacola, Kent, Watkins Glen, Greenwood, Meadowdale, Road America, and Bridgehampton.

1964

Carol Conners wrote and sang a song, "Hey Little Cobra,"
that added to the popularity of Shelby's creation.

"Hey, I really liked listening to it!"

After the triumph at Sebring, Shelby American had a good start toward winning the World Manufacturers' Championship. Le Mans, of course, was the big one. Dan Gurney and Bob Bondurant (shown) took a Daytona Coupe to 4th overall and 1st in GT, the highest placed Cobra.

The Ford Motor Company entered three of its new Ford GTs (GT-40) in the 1964 Le Mans. The drivers were Richie Ginther/Masten Gregory (#11, shown), Phil Hill/Bruce McLaren, and Richard Attwood/Jo Schlesser.

All three cars failed to finish due to various mechanical problems.

1964

During 1964, Ford Advanced Vehicles, based in England, entered the new Ford GTs. The final race of the season was Nassau. Two cars were entered, but both failed to finish because of improper maintenance and preparation. That year the team failed to win a single race.

1964

Due to the GTs' lack of success, Ford turned to Shelby for help. Two cars were delivered to Shelby American in December 1964. According to John Ohlsen, "Both cars were a mess. We had to start working immediately, because there was a lot to do to get ready for the next year's first event at Daytona, which was scheduled for February."

1964

1965

"Right out of the box, Shelby American scored the first victory for the Ford GT at the February 28, 1965, Daytona. My drivers were Ken Miles and Lloyd Ruby."

"My Shelby American team at Daytona (left to right):
Ken Miles, me, Lloyd Ruby, Leo Beebe, and Ray Geddes."

1965

When Ford came out with the Mustang in 1965, its creator, Lee Iacocca, wanted to have a car that could compete with GM's Corvette. So he asked Carroll Shelby to perform the same magic that he had done with the AC. Two versions were designed: "S" for touring and "R" for racing. The racing version received the 300-bhp Cobra engine and a number of other modifications.

"I introduced my new GT-350 at Riverside Raceway on
January 27, 1965, to enthusiastic reviews from the press.
We made 12 Rs and 550 Ss that year."

1965

"We at Shelby American had a lot on our plate during 1965: developing, testing, racing, and making 350 Mustangs; 289 Cobras; and 427 Cobras, Daytona Coupes, King Cobras, and Ford GTs. Our facility in Venice was bursting at the seams."

1965

Ken Miles and Bruce McLaren drove this Shelby American–entered Ford GT to win the Prototype GT +4000 class at the March 27, 1965, 12 Hours of Sebring. They finished 2nd overall to Jim Hall and Hap Sharp in Hall's Chaparral 2A. As dusk approached, rain swept over the course.

McLaren remarked, "Ken and I appreciated that our car had a roof."

The 1965 SCCA U.S. Road Racing Championship at Laguna Seca on May 9 was hotly contested, as this photo shows. Ken Miles (#98), Ed Leslie (#96), and Bob Johnson (#97) are in Cobras.

"My Shelby American team won the Grand Turismo category for the third year in a row."

1965

Carroll Shelby and Henry Ford II came to the 1965 Le Mans with high hopes. After all, it was the era of the Ford-Ferrari wars. Five Ford GTs and five Shelby Daytonas were entered. Phil Hill, in a Ford, set a new track record of 3 minutes, 33 seconds at 142.25 mph. But even so, because of engine problems, all five GTs failed to finish.

"I teamed Ken Miles and Bruce McLaren in the Ford GT MKII #1. They led the 1965 Le Mans for the first 2 hours, but then had to quit with a broken gearbox." Here, Miles leads the Peter Sutcliff/Peter Harper Daytona Coupe through the Mulsanne hairpin.

1965

The only Daytona to finish (in 7th) at the 1965 Le Mans was driven by Dr. Dick Thompson and Jack Sears (#11).

1965

In late 1965, Goodyear asked Shelby for the use of a Daytona Coupe for five-time World Land-Speed Record holder Craig Breedlove to run at Bonneville. The car was called *Sonic 1*. Breedlove drove it to 23 class speed and endurance records.

"I have always been affiliated with Goodyear."

"In 1965, my Shelby American won the World Manufacturers' Championship. It was the first time an American company had won. The title was clinched at Reims where my team ran two Cobras, one driven by Sir John Whitmore (left) and Jack Sears. The other was driven by Bob Bondurant (in car) and Jo Schlesser."

1965

1966

Shelby started 1966 with a bang. Ken Miles (touching the trophy) and Lloyd Ruby (left) won the Daytona Continental 24 Hour in February in a Shelby American Ford GT MK IIB.

"The event was a triumph for me and for Shelby American. The Fords finished 1st, 2nd, and 3rd. Dan Gurney and Jerry Grant were 2nd with Walt Hansgen and Mark Donohue 3rd. Bruce McLaren and Chris Amon were 5th in another Shelby Ford."

"I [right] entered Dan Gurney [left] and Jerry Grant as well as Ken Miles and Lloyd Ruby in the March 1966 12 Hours of Sebring in Ford GTs. Dan and Jerry led for almost the entire race, but their car broke down on the last lap.

Dan and I are longtime
close friends."

This shot captures the running start of the 1966 12 Hours of Sebring.
Dan Gurney is about to jump into the Shelby Ford GT in the foreground.

1966

Ken Miles (left) and Lloyd Ruby (right) were following the leading Gurney/Grant Ford GT at the 1966 Sebring. So when the Gurney/Grant car dropped out, Miles and Ruby took the checkered flag.

1966

Next, it was off to France for the Shelby American team for the 1966 24 Hours of Le Mans. Here, Shelby (in a business suit) and Ken Miles are in front of the Bruce McLaren/Chris Amon Ford GT with some of the crew in the background.

"I assigned Walt Hansgen to drive one of my Ford GTs at the 1966 Le Mans. When Walt went out during practice, it was drizzling rain. I told him to be very careful and to take it easy. Nevertheless, he went faster and faster."

Then he fishtailed before the Dunlop Turn. Trying to go into the escape road, he hit a bank, skidded, and flipped end over end. He suffered severe injuries and died in the hospital. *"What a tragedy!"*

1966

1966

The start of the 1966 Le Mans: Dan Gurney is running toward Ford #3 and Ken Miles toward #1. Henry Ford II is at bottom right in a suit holding a flag.

At the start, Graham Hill, in an Alan Mann–entered Ford GT, led, but after three laps, Dan Gurney took the lead. For the next 5 hours, either the Gurney/Grant or the Miles/Hulme Ford GT was in front. When the sun came up on Sunday, the first four cars were Ford GTs, but then the Gurney/Grant car blew its head gasket leaving three. *"Toward the end, Ken Miles and Denny Hulme were in front followed by the Bruce McLaren/Chris Amon Ford GT with the Ronnie Bucknum/Dick Hutcherson Ford GT about 60 miles behind the two leaders."*

1966

Henry Ford II
wanted a dead-heat
finish.

But this was not possible because of the staggered start. McLaren/Amon won because they started behind Miles and so traveled farther. On the last lap, Ken Miles and Bruce McLaren were on the same lap, so they slowed down and waited for the Bucknum/Hutcherson Ford to catch up. Miles was leading with McLaren 2nd and Bucknum 3rd. Just before the finish line, Miles slowed down and allowed McLaren to take the checkered flag. *"I was upset with Ford and sorry for Ken; but what could I do? I couldn't say anything. The Deuce was the boss."*

1966

On August 17, 1966, the unspeakable happened. Ken Miles was killed at Riverside while testing a prototype new Ford GT called the "J Car." It was a tragedy, not only for Carroll Shelby personally and the Shelby American team, but also for my family and me. Our two families were very close. Ken and my dad, Art Evans Sr. (right), were best friends and Ken's wife, Mollie, was a close friend of my stepmother. At Mollie's request, my dad delivered the eulogy at Ken's service. Ken and Mollie's son, Peter, became part of my family and still is.

Meanwhile, back at the factory, the 1966 GT350 Shelby fastbacks were on sale and customers were racing them in the SCCA B-Production class. Hertz was buying the GT350H models as rental cars. Specifications for the 1967 GT350 and the new GT500 models were finalized in August 1966. In September, production began at the Los Angeles International Airport facility. By November, cars were being delivered to Ford dealers nationwide. *"My Shelby American had turned into a big business!"*

1966

1967

The first race of 1967 was the 24 Hours of Daytona on February 4–5. It was a disaster for the Ford GTs. All had transmission problems and couldn't stay put together (without Ken Miles!); five of the six entries were withdrawn. Chris Amon, in a Ferrari 330 P3 (#23), won. Here, Amon is followed by Dan Gurney in a Shelby American Ford GT MKII and another Ferrari.

"My team really felt the loss of Ken. And, of course, it hit me personally then and still does."

The Shelby American team talks it over: (clockwise) Lucien Bianchi (back to camera), Bruce McLaren, Dan Gurney, A. J. Foyt, Frank Gardner, Ronnie Bucknum, Al Dowd, and Carroll Shelby.

"I have to say that we had assembled a really great team, even without Ken."

Developed during the previous winter, Shelby American entered the new Ford GT Mk IV at the April 1, 1967, 12 Hours of Sebring.

1967

"I assigned Mario Andretti and Bruce McLaren to drive the new Ford GT Mk IV at the 1967 Sebring. They won. After the race, Mario told me, 'We had a hell of a battle with the Chaparral. The Mk IV is fantastic. I was involved with testing and I think we are ready for Le Mans.'"

At the start, the two Fords took the lead with the Shelby entry leading the Holman & Moody car. Mike Spence, in the Chaparral, took the lead by the quarter distance and set the fastest lap of the race at 111.032 mph. But on the 145th lap, the Chaparral's differential failed, leaving the Fords 1st and 2nd. Until the 226th lap, the two Fords were running nose to tail. But then, the engine blew in the Holman & Moody entry. Even so, Foyt and Ruby had put in more laps than all others except the Shelby American. So Andretti (left) and McLaren (right) won at the 12th hour having put in 238 laps.

1967

Next was the 1967 24 Hours of Le Mans. The Shelby American crew (left to right): Steve Schthack, Phil Henry, Dennis Cragg, Max Kelley, Charlie Agapiou, Gordon Chance, Gary Koike, Dick Wilson, John Collins, and Ron Butler. *"I entered Dan Gurney and A. J. Foyt plus Bruce McLaren and Mark Donohue in MK IVs as well as Ronnie Bucknum and Paul Hawkins in a MK IIB."* Others brought 8 more Ford GTs, making a total of 11. *"But only 2 finished; both were mine and they were in 1st and 2nd."*

1967

1967

At the start of the 1967 24 Hours of Le Mans, Ronnie Bucknum led in the Shelby American Ford GT MK IIB (#57) followed by the Shelby American Ford GT MK IV (#1) driven by Dan Gurney (pulling out just behind Bucknum). The Bruce McLaren/Mark Donohue Shelby American Ford GT MK IV (#2) is at the left with Jim Hall's Chaparral next. *Jim and I have been close friends for many years. Also, he is very, very smart.*

Shelby (wearing cap) watches over a pit stop during the 1967 24 Hours of Le Mans.

A. J. Foyt (barely visible) is driving the winning Shelby American Ford GT MK IV toward Victory Lane. Sitting on the front of the car are Dan Gurney, who is waving, and across from him, team mechanic Mike Donovan, who is holding a Jeroboam of champagne. Crew Chief John Collins is sitting behind Donovan; behind Collins are Phil Henny and then Charlie Agapiou. *"This victory was due, not only to the drivers, but also my great crew."*

1967

"In 1967, I decided that I wanted to compete in the Can-Am. I had a car built that I named 'King Cobra.' It was designed by Len Terry of Lotus and constructed by Phil Remington, one of my great workers."

It was completed around August.

Power was from a 325-ci Ford with Gurney-Westlake heads and Weber carburetors. The problem was that it didn't handle well and a small-block engine powered it while its competition had big-blocks, so it was also down on power. Jerry Titus crashed it during the season's last Can-Am at Las Vegas. Afterward, Shelby ditched the effort.

In 1966, the SCCA started a professional series, the Trans-American Sedan Championship. Ford executive Roy Geddes asked Shelby to field a team of GT350 Mustangs.

In this photo, Jerry Titus, in a GT350, is leading John McComb, in another Mustang, at Riverside.

1967

During 1967, 12 Trans-Am events were held. Jerry Titus (left) won 5 of them and came in 3rd in 2. The Shelby American team was instrumental in Ford winning the championship that year.

"During 1967, my Shelby American was going full-speed ahead turning out Shelby Mustangs that were sold by selected Ford dealers. That year we built more than 3,000; 1,174 were GT350s and 2,947 were GT500s. I was lucky to have some really great guys to keep it going."

"Jerry Titus (#17, at Mid-Ohio) led my 1967 Shelby Trans-Am team. My other drivers were Dr. Dick Thompson and Ronnie Bucknum."

1967

In 1967, Carroll Shelby wanted a car to demonstrate Goodyear's new Thunderbolt budget passenger-car tires at a high-profile press event, but the mission was expanded after a chance encounter between Shelby and his friend, former Shelby American sales manager, Don McCain. McCain suggested that Carroll put a racing 427 Le Mans Ford GT engine in a GT500 for the test and let him sell the car with the intention of building 50 more. They would then be marketed and sold to the public as the powerhouse Shelby Super Snakes.

Shelby instructed Fred Goodell, Shelby American's chief engineer (who was on loan from Ford), to prepare the GT500 with a special engine for the test. McCain described it as "the mother of all 600-bhp 427s"; it powered the car to a top speed of 170 mph with Shelby at the wheel for press demonstration laps. The event was judged a success, but McCain's plan to sell 50 Super Snakes was ultimately dashed by the car's $8,000 price tag; only three were built; *$8,000 was a lot of money then!*

1967

1968

The last year that Cobras were produced by Shelby American was 1968. AC Cars kept accurate production records that show a total of 998 chassis were manufactured. Of course, since then, a good number have been built by others. However, in the view of purists, these are not legitimate. Here, Cobra guru Lynn Park is shown driving his 427.

Beginning in 1967 and continuing through 1970, Toyota produced and sold a sports car, the 2000GT.
In 1968, the SCCA accepted 2000GTs as production cars and, therefore, eligible to run in the C-Production class.

1968

1968

"Toyota contracted with me to compete in SCCA races in order to promote sales. I hired Davey Jordan and Scooter Patrick to drive them for me."

Jordan (shown) and Patrick were both experienced drivers. Davey had won the 1967 SCCA C-Production championship driving a 911 Porsche. Scooter was the SCCA National Champion in 1966. Even though the SCCA races were supposed to be amateur, the two drivers were each paid $400 plus expenses per weekend. Shelby fielded a serious effort with a large professional crew. At the end of the 1968 season, Scooter was 3rd in the SCCA Southern Pacific Division with Davey 4th. All in all, they ran in 14 events. Scooter was 1st twice, 3rd three times, and 4th four times. Davey scored two 1sts, four 2nds, and three 3rds. Toyota didn't renew the contract with Shelby for 1969.

1968

"In 1967, I hired an engineer, Ken Wallis, to design a turbine-powered car for the 1968 Indy 500. Two cars were completed. I assigned Denny Hulme and Bruce McLaren (shown) to drive. During testing, they were coming up to competitive speeds and looked as if they might be a threat. But due to a dispute regarding their legality, I was forced to withdraw the team; I decided to abandon the project."

In 1968, Shelby introduced the first Shelby Mustang convertible.

Shelby Mustangs were no longer made in California; construction was farmed out to A. O. Smith in Michigan. Shelby Mustangs were no longer selling well.

1968

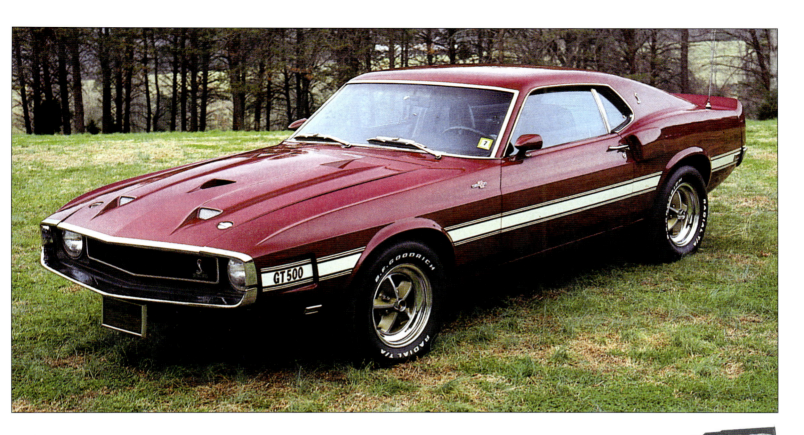

The end of the decade experienced a slow decline of Shelby American. Production ended in September 1969.

In May 1969, Sam Posey won the Trans-Am at Lime Rock driving a Shelby Mustang entered by the Shelby Racing Company. It was the last win of the Shelby American era. Sam told me: "That was one hell of a race. The engine was running on seven for the last half hour and the Bud Moore cars were closing in on me. After the flag, Lew Spencer had to haul me out of the car; I couldn't stand up."

1968

1970s

This 1970 Shelby Mustang GT500 was one of the last built until the modern era.

Originally, it was an unsold 1969 model that was updated to 1970 specifications. When Ford took over production from Shelby American, they moved further and further away from Carroll Shelby's original concept. I talked to him about it during the summer of 2010. He told me, *"They got heavier and heavier and, because of this, were no longer competitive as far as racing was concerned. They weighed more than 3,000 pounds."* In 1969, Shelby announced that he was retiring. A total of 601 Shelby GT350 and GT500 cars were produced as 1970 models. Shelby American and the Shelby Racing Company went out of business at the end of 1969.

"In 1970, I decided to explore Africa, including Botswana, Angola, and the Central African Republic. I spent approximately nine months of every year there during the 1970s."

Shelby even led some big-game hunting safaris. When I asked him why, he replied, *"I just wanted to see it."* Some years later, he expressed regrets for having killed elephants. During that time, he maintained a home in Vista del Mar and then Playa del Rey, California.

In January 1973, Shelby established the Shelby Wheel Company, headquartered in Gardena, California. The company manufactured and distributed aftermarket specialty wheels.

Carroll Shelby was a fan of chili. In fact, he was one of the founders of the world's first Championship Chili Cookoff held in Terlingua, Texas, in 1967. At the 1972 cookoff, Shelby announced that his Original Texas Brand Chili Mix was on the market. Although he sold it to Kraft Foods in 1986, Shelby's world-famous mix is a favorite of chili connoisseurs everywhere, with four individual spice packets that let you season to taste 2 pounds of beef or poultry.

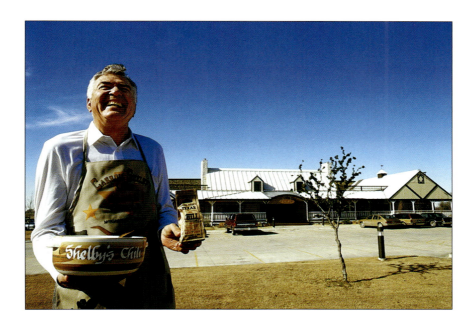

Carroll Shelby's Chili combines a blend of the robust, hearty taste of East Texas with the flavorful, often eye-watering spices of Old Mexico.

The ingredients are Cayenne pepper, masa (corn flour), cumin, garlic, ground chili peppers, onion, oregano, paprika, and salt. You can buy it in many grocery stores as well as online. Shelby is seen here with a bowl of his chili at his ranch house in Texas.

1980s

"During the 1980s, I had a relationship with Chrysler to develop 'Shelbyized' Dodges. The first was the 1983–1984 Dodge Shelby Charger. Rather than focusing on speed, I had my crew modify the suspension and styling."

Production was 8,251 the first year and 7,552 the following year. This car is in Shelby's private collection. In 1985–1987, 16,389 Shelby Chargers were built with turbocharged engines. During the 1980s, Chrysler sold many more cars with the Shelby name than Ford did during the 1960s.

From Chrysler's standpoint, the tie-in with Shelby was golden. But the cars have never been particularly desirable for collectors. They do not fetch stratospheric figures at auctions, as do other Shelby cars. This photo by Carl Goodwin shows Shelby with a Charger engine.

Shelby Chargers were raced extensively. Joe Varde campaigned this one in the IMSA Champion Spark Plug Challenge. In racing trim, the engine produced 180 bhp at 7,500 rpm and ran 0-60 in 5.9 seconds and the quarter-mile in 14.3 seconds. It had a top speed of 144 mph.

Shelby offered an optional C/S Handling Package to Dodge Daytona owners through licensed Shelby dealers. In 1986, 5,984 customers ordered this package. A "Shelby" version of the Daytona was introduced in 1987 and named the Dodge Daytona Z. It was available with the Turbo II engine, a heavy-duty transaxle, and Getrag gears.

Shelby offered an aftermarket kit to his licensed dealers for the Dodge Durango sport-utility vehicle. It was called the Shelby SP 360. During Shelby's time with Chrysler, a total of 22 different Shelby Dodge or Dodge Shelby models were offered.

1980s

"In 1989, I tried to bring back the Can-Am Series using a spec car (meaning that all entrants used the same model). I built 76 of these Dodge Can-Ams using my race version of the Chrysler 3.3L V-6 engine that put out 225 hp."

All were sold as kits. The concept failed to catch on in the United States; the SCCA didn't re-introduce the series. However, a successful series using these cars was instituted in South Africa.

In 1989, Shelby began production of 427 S/C Cobras using "leftover" serial numbers from 1966. Initially, he announced that he had "found" a number of old Cobra chassis. A few were sold, but then the California DMV questioned the dates of origin and the project was abandoned.

1990s to Present

In 1990, Shelby had an "end-stage heart failure." He was in line for a heart transplant, but he got weaker and weaker and was finally hospitalized. Eventually, a heart became available from a man who had died in Las Vegas. Shelby's heart surgeon, Alfred Trento, flew to Vegas for the donor heart. When he removed Shelby's heart, he noted that Shelby had had at least 40 heart attacks! He remarked that he had never seen such a heart that was still pumping.

After the operation, Shelby's body had a continuing problem with rejecting the new heart, which required a great deal of very expensive medication. To combat rejection, the medication had to be changed frequently for the rest of Shelby's life. On a number of occasions, I can remember Shel telling me that he had to go to the hospital to receive different medication.

While Shelby was awaiting a new heart, he met a young child whose heart had been affected by a virus.

The boy visited Shelby numerous times while they both waited. He had a profound effect on Shelby.

"After I recovered from the operation, I established the Carroll Shelby Children's Foundation, whose aim was to help recipient children to afford the expensive and lifelong necessity for medication. Many children's families cannot afford it and they will die without it.

"Initially, I was personally involved in the selection of children who received my help. The first recipient was an infant named Leah Smith who needed a transplant in 1991. She was within days of dying because her parents couldn't afford the medication."

Leah survived, thanks to the Foundation and, as a teenager, she became a champion ice skater and ballroom dancer. She even made her way to the Olympic trials.

The Foundation is supported by donations. Shelby, himself, has donated and added his appearance fees and autograph fees. More than 95 percent of receipts go to beneficiaries with only 5 percent being used for administration. The Foundation is located at Shelby's Gardena facility, where no office rent or overhead is charged.

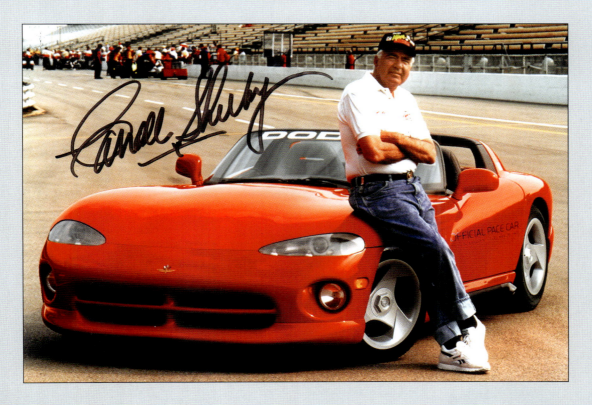

In 1991, Shelby drove the pace car at the Indy 500. It was a Dodge Viper and his passenger was my friend and West Point classmate Norm Schwarzkopf. Norm remarked, "I wasn't scared in combat, but someone arranged for me to have a ride around Indy. The driver was a pretty old guy and while we were cruising around the track at 140 mph, he told me he had just come back from the hospital where he had a heart transplant."

"*In 1999, I went back into the Cobra business and introduced a new 427 S/C series* (starting with serial number CXS 4000)." He began building them at the Nevada Territorial Prison, putting prisoners to work. Soon, however, he moved the operation to a shop at the new Las Vegas Motor Speedway.

Shelby's Las Vegas factory continues to turn out Cobras as well as Shelby Mustangs, with new models announced every year. The Ford factory ships Mustangs to Las Vegas where they are transformed into Shelbys. A Shelby Mustang is the top of the line at selected Ford dealers. The legendary Shelby Mustang GT-H (originally made for Hertz) was resurrected in 2006.

The Shelby Series 1 was designed from the ground up and produced by Shelby.

1990s to Present

The cars had either supercharged or normally aspirated Oldsmobile engines. The supercharged versions were fitted with larger brakes and a heavy-duty clutch. Performance was 0-60 mph in 3.2 seconds. A total of 249 were built, all 1999 models.

On a very special day in April 2001, we had a birthday party for Jack Brabham at my home in Redondo Beach. A number of very special people were there to help us celebrate (left to right): Phil Hill, Rodger Ward, Carroll Shelby, Jack Brabham, and Dan Gurney. Phil led us in singing "Happy Birthday." Afterward, Shelby remarked, *Never again will all of us be together.* He was right.

Every June since the late 1950s, a bunch of us old timers have a party at the Bothwell Ranch. Shelby was always there. In this photo taken in 2001, he is with Ann Bothwell (center) and Sam Hank's widow, Alice.

In July 2004, we had a party at the Bothwell Ranch. Shelby was there with Bill Murphy (right). Murf, as we called him, had a long relationship with Shelby. They were partners in a car dealership, Murphy & Shelby Dodge in San Fernando, near Los Angeles. Bill Murphy died on July 14, 2005. Shelby hosted a tribute to Murphy at the Bel-Air Country Club. Shel asked me to speak about Murf, which I was privileged to do.

1990s to Present

Mary Davis and Shelby got together at the Bothwell Ranch in June 2010. Mary Davis, a driver during the 1950s, built and operated the famous Portofino Inn in Redondo Beach. The inn was a favorite of many racing luminaries including Mario Andretti and Bobby Unser.

1990s to Present

Shelby was particularly fond of children. He and my grandson, Austin, had a very special relationship. I took this photo of them on July 6, 2010.

1990s to Present

Three old friends got together at John and Ginny Dixon's Palos Verdes Estates home on January 6, 2011, to celebrate. All had birthdays in January and all raced in California during the 1950s (left to right): Carroll Shelby, me, and Herb Jones. Herb moved to England in the mid-1960s and raced there.

1990s to Present

The last car with which Shelby was involved was the 2013 Shelby Mustang GT500, introduced in the fall of the previous year.

With 662 bhp and 631 ft-lbs of torque, it can hit 60 mph in 3.5 seconds and does the quarter-mile in 11.6 seconds. It's a fitting conclusion to such an incredible career.

For the last 10 years of Shelby's life, he and my son, David, were very close. David took care of Shelby's personal car collection and they went everywhere together. David even had his own bedroom in Shelby's Bel Air house. In late 2011, when Shelby became ill, David took him to and from the hospital. David was one of the very few people that Shelby allowed to see him in the hospital.

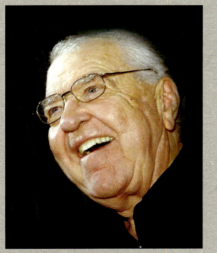

On May 10, 2012, Carroll Hall Shelby died after a six-month illness. At the end of November 2011, he was in and out of the hospital a number of times. This went on until the New Year, when he became so ill that he couldn't return home anymore.

About two weeks before he died, his sons, Michael and Patrick, came to the hospital in Los Angeles and took him home to Dallas, where they put him in the Baylor University Hospital. This is where he died.

During the months of his hospitalization in Los Angeles, Shelby didn't want anyone to visit him other than his wife Cleo and David. He didn't want anyone to see him in the condition he was in. Shelby and I talked via cell phone and I repeatedly told him I wanted to visit. As far as I know, the only person who did visit was his longtime employee, Tracey Smith.

During our telephone conversations, we talked about a number of things, including this pictorial odyssey. He was eager for me to put it all together. As it turned out, it took more than a year after his passing for me to complete it. I wanted to get it right; Shelby would have approved.

When he passed on at Baylor, his children surrounded him: Sharon, Michael, and Patrick. He was survived by the three children, several grandchildren, and six of his seven wives. His first wife, Jeanne, lived in Dallas along with the three children. I never met her, but we talked occasionally by telephone. The last time I called, her caregiver told me that she was so ill she couldn't come to the phone. Jeanne died on October 12, 2012. The children lost both their parents in the same year.

This photo by Tracey Smith depicts Carroll Shelby the way I want to remember him.

1990s to Present

Even with Shelby gone, the Carroll Shelby Foundation lives on. Its mission is "Dedicated to providing financial support for children and medical professionals to help overcome life-threatening health issues worldwide and promoting continuing educational development."

Following years of heart-related difficulties that culminated in a successful heart transplant, Shelby created the Carroll Shelby Children's Foundation in October 1991. The organization is dedicated to providing assistance for acute coronary and kidney care for young people who share many of the same afflictions as Shelby. In 2009, the foundation took another step and expanded its reach to become the Carroll Shelby Foundation, helping children from their first heartbeat through their education years.

The Foundation has helped numerous youngsters undergo major coronary surgeries and helps charities and children worldwide to raise money for their own funding campaigns.

In addition to providing seed money to launch healthcare programs and facilities, the Foundation also provides grants to organizations conducting research in the fields of coronary and organ transplant management. The Foundation provides scholarship money to children dedicated to enhancing their lives through continuing educational opportunities in the automotive field.

Shelby, who waited years before receiving his own heart transplant, was keenly aware of the difficulties and expense involved in heart surgery and the often-lengthy process to locate a suitable donor organ. He created the Foundation because he realized that many needy children would have their lives cut short without some type of financial assistance.

Please consider making a donation to help support the cause so dear to Shelby's heart. The Foundation is a 501 (c) 3 charity and your donation is tax deductible. Make your check payable to "The Carroll Shelby Foundation" and mail it to 19021 S. Figueroa St., Gardena, CA 90248.

1990s to Present

Carroll Hall Shelby's legacy lives on: Shelby American in Las Vegas builds a variety of models of Shelby Mustangs and Cobras as well as aftermarket speed parts and accessories. For more information, go to Shelby.com.

Art Evans, Co-Author

Art Evans began road racing during the 1950s. His first race was in an MG at Palm Springs in 1955. Soon, he acquired an MG Special and then a succession of XK-120 Jaguars that he raced in Southern California. At the end of the decade, he campaigned the first Devin SS.

During the 1950s, he and his partner, OCee Ritch, owned a public relations and advertising company that represented the MG Mitten Company, Devin Enterprises, Gough Industries, and other car-related organizations.

Evans and another partner, Richard Sherwin, published the monthly *Sports Car Journal*. Evans served as a director of the Los Angeles Region of the Sports Car Club of America and was involved in publishing a number of 1950s-era event programs. His Evans Industries became the exclusive

Photo by Will Edgar.

distributor for Devin cars and products. He and Bill Devin were essentially partners as well as lifelong friends.

Art Evans taught for a year in middle school, a year in high school, and then was the Chair of the Photography Department at Orange Coast College for six years. Following that, he pursued directing and producing motion pictures for 10 years at Paramount Pictures.

As a cinematographer, Art worked on commercials that featured Mario Andretti and John Fitch. His still photographs have been displayed in numerous exhibitions, including a solo at Lincoln Center in New York City. Art has taken portraits of racing personalities, including Sir Stirling Moss, Sir Jack Brabham, Bobby Unser, Phil Hill, Dan Gurney, Carroll Shelby, and John Fitch. A number of these photos have been published in various magazines and books.

Evans is the author of several books about motorsports. He started with a series about road racing during the 1950s. Then he wrote *Ken Miles*, the only biography of that great driver. Next was another series recounting the histories of road races at California venues: Pebble Beach, Golden Gate, Paramount Ranch, and Torrey Pines. Art wrote two books about Carroll Shelby: *Shelby, the Race Driver* and *The Shelby American Story*. He also co-authored two books with John Fitch: *Racing With Mercedes* and *Racing Corvette: The Early Years*. His articles have appeared in such periodicals as *AutoWeek*, *Vintage Motorsport*, *Victory Lane*, *Vintage Racecar*, *Vintage Oval Racing*, and *Sports Car Digest*.

During the 1980s, Art began driving in vintage races. In 1985, he promoted a revival of the old Palm Springs Road Races followed by a succession of other events, including a vintage section at the Pikes Peak International Hill Climb and open-road racing in Mexico.

The Evans family lives in Redondo Beach, California. In retirement, Art pursues pastimes including writing about motorsports and serving as the secretary and newsletter editor of The Fabulous Fifties Association.

Art Evans, Co-Author

Art Evans in the
Devin SS (#93) at
Santa Barbara in 1959.

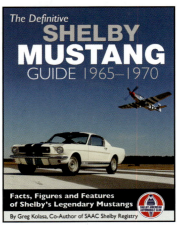
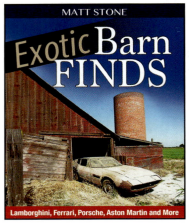
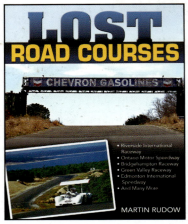
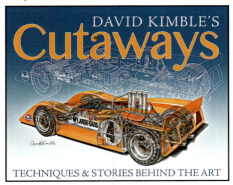